FROM BRICKS TO CLICKS

FROM BRICKS TO CLICKS

A guide to selling on-line.

BY DAVE BURNETT

From Bricks to Clicks by Dave Burnett

This is a work of fiction. Names, characters, places, and incidents either are the products of the author's imagination or are used fictitiously. Any resemblance to actual persons, living or dead, businesses, companies, events, or locales is entirely coincidental.

Although every precaution has been taken to verify the accuracy of the information contained herein, the author and publisher assume no responsibility for any errors or omissions. No liability is assumed for damages that may result from the use of information contained within.

Published by: An Opportunity Knocks

Books may be purchased by contacting the publisher and author at:
Dave Burnett | AOK Marketing Group | db@AOKMG.com |

First Edition

Cover and Interior Design: Tanya Bäck Designs
Copyeditor: Chris Atchison

ISBN# 978-0-9958526-0-0

10 9 8 7 6 5 4 3 2 1

To my amazing wife Mary.
Thank you for putting up with all my crazy ideas and
sticking with me on this serial entrepreneur's journey.
I couldn't be where I am today without you.

To my wonderful kids, Mark and Christina.
You are what makes my day special and what drives me to
be a better person. I am so grateful you are in my life, and
hopefully this book shows you that you can do anything you
want if you work hard enough, and you want it bad enough.

Contents

Foreword

In the time that it takes you to read this sentence, you've lost a potential customer.

It's a fact that's frustrated me for a long time. No, let me rephrase that: It's a reality of online marketing that makes me angry. Small to medium-sized businesses are sabotaging their online success through their negligence when it comes to their digital marketing strategy—assuming they have one, and most don't.

Let me be clear. When people visit your website, they want to do one of four things: they want to know, they want to go, they want to interact, or they want to buy.

These are the basic transactional realities of our digital world. When a customer or audience member visits a website or social media page—any online platform, really—they'll inevitably want to achieve one of these four goals. Once they arrive at their desired digital destination, they'll demand that the information be accurate, immediately available and detailed enough to satisfy their needs.

In other words, they're impatient and demand to have game-changing, universally accessible information at their fingertips in a nanosecond. If you can't satisfy their demands, you've failed as an online marketer because in our era of real-time digital communication, availability is part of relevancy. Potential customers won't give your organization the benefit of the doubt if your website looks terrible or your blog hasn't been updated in five years. Give them what they want—no, *impress* them—or they will bounce off your website. It's as simple as that.

This isn't simply a challenge—it's a nightmare scenario for any organization, be it business-to-consumer (B2C) or business-to-business (B2B) focused.

So, why is it that so many companies simply ignore the very basic tenets of 21st century online marketing? As a digital marketer for more than two decades and a founder of four technology/marketing start-ups, I've interacted with hundreds of B2B and B2C clients over the years. With the exception of a relative handful, nearly all of them fell short when it came to marketing their companies online. That list includes Fortune 500 firms that have the resources and manpower to blow the doors off of their competition, at least when it comes to search engine optimization (SEO), branding, content marketing and other initiatives. But they still mostly fail in the endeavour.

So, here's why I founded my current business, AOK Marketing.

I previously owned and operated a promotional products company—the third start-up of my career after founding a product sampling business and the popular digital employee rewards platform I Love Rewards, now Achievers.com—that was performing well until late 2007. Then the U.S. economy collapsed as the Great Recession of 2008-09 tightened its grip on global economies. I needn't remind those of you who lived through that unpleasant time what a disaster it was. When the global economy essentially collapsed and desperate companies slashed everything from employee headcount to marketing budgets, promotional item purchases were some of the first line items on the chopping block. Our company was losing more than $70,000 per month at the recession's peak, and our fiscal momentum was going in the wrong direction. We would be dead by the end of the year if something didn't change.

It finally happened when I looked for a new way to market our business, a complete Hail Mary pass to restore revenue.

Ironically, even though our competitors were marketers by trade, they were doing a terrible job promoting their brands online. About 50 per cent of the industry didn't have a website or were using website templates that were difficult to navigate or customize. In fact, most were barely searchable. The majority of promotional item companies lacked proper website contact information—instead relying on shady toll free numbers—and didn't bother to set up Google profiles that would create a listing of their business to help customers find their websites online.

None of our competitors opened social media accounts or set up profiles, let alone broadcasting on those channels, which at that point were still new but becoming increasingly popular. None were defending their brands online (I wish I could say trademark protection was an after-thought, but it wasn't a thought in the first place), they weren't analyzing competitor activities and certainly weren't responsive to the growing surge in mobile surfing and e-commerce. In short, they were doing almost nothing to appeal to search engines such as Google, let alone their customers.

Our team viewed these shortcomings as the perfect opportunity to learn from our competitors' mistakes and do online marketing the right way. It started when we purchased 3,000 domain names, set up basic websites and optimized each of them for search. We watched, waited and tracked our results, tweaking search engine marketing tactics along the way. Within about six months, our sales began to rebound and the worst of our recession-driven financial malaise seemed to be behind us.

Then, something interesting happened. Our competitors finally began to take note of our increasing market share. Every time they queried common search terms related to the promotional items industry, they kept finding our company. I began receiving calls from rivals looking for help. They wanted us to assist with their website design, search engine optimization and marketing. Being the competitive entrepreneur that I am, I told the first five callers to take a hike. By the sixth call the magical lightbulb in my brain suddenly switched on. Call it a revelation, or an A-HA moment, but I realized their requests weren't so outrageous, after all. What if we formed a side business to provide online marketing services to our competitors, then expanded that service offering to include companies of all sizes across sectors?

Thanks to the fortuitous collision of necessity and demand, we embraced an entirely different business model and haven't looked back since. But that doesn't explain why our competitors were marketing so poorly in the first place. As we've seen over the years, it's not a problem limited to the promotional items sector. I would argue that organizations tend to drop the online marketing ball due, at least in part, to a set of common missteps and challenges. There are many, so I'll only list my top three below.

For a start, many fail to allot adequate budgets to implement their marketing campaigns, both online and off. I can't overestimate the number of clients I've worked with in the past who were determined to market their products or services and had truly dynamic ideas of exactly how to do it—until the issue of price arose. The fact that their plans might cost hundreds of thousands of dollars, or more, to deploy seemed to be a shocking revelation. The senior leaders holding the purse strings in the background weren't prepared to shell out cash to make these plans happen. It's no secret that marketing costs money—sometimes lots of it—but many organizations fail to make that connection and instead hope to minimize their budget spend. Going cheap on marketing almost always leads to failure and subsequent re-investment to do the job right a second time.

Next, they understaff the project, assuming they haven't gone the outsourcing route and contracted a third-party provider to handle the job. We've all met an overworked marketing team—you may even be part of one. They're the group ordered by their ambitious business owner, CMO or marketing manager to roll out a huge campaign, only to watch the whole thing fall flat when it becomes obvious that doing too much with too few people is a recipe for failure. As with most business initiatives, marketing projects need to be properly staffed if they have any chance of being successful. But again, these budgets are the first area where organizations attempt to cut spending, so too often a handful of marketing staffers are asked to do the work of a dozen or more.

But even when companies do have strong marketing budgets and adequate staff, they often spend their precious funds in the wrong places. One notorious area, at least for B2B organizations, is social media. Yes, I said it: social media is often an inefficient way to spend precious marketing dollars—and that's from a CEO whose company manages social media accounts on behalf of more than 100 clients. Our team has found that unless your company is marketing social media services of some sort, these platforms are virtually useless for generating and converting sales leads. Their real utility is in building brand awareness and making existing customers more loyal.

Many organizations also fail to do the research necessary to understand their target audience or clientele, leading them to spend their marketing budgets in the most inefficient or ineffective ways possible. I've seen small to medium-sized businesses spend a relative fortune to exhibit at trade shows, for example—pouring money into everything from booth design and exhibition fees, to on-site marketing—only to acquire few or no sales in return. Why? Because they failed to do the necessary legwork to develop a coherent strategy before the event to acquire a highly targeted customer segment, build a database of leads during the show, then work to convert those leads into new customers afterwards. And that's just one way companies fall short on the marketing front. Others might spend thousands on ineffective online advertising campaigns and glean similarly poor results.

Lastly, most companies that I've encountered aren't doing nearly enough to build effective websites. Here's the thing: a website should be any organization's best sales tool. I want every marketing manager/coordinator/CEO/social media coordinator/digital acquisition specialist who reads this book to ask themselves a very simple question: Do we have a website traffic problem, or a website conversion problem? Most organizations look at their website from an aesthetic or SEO standpoint, and that's OK. Both are important considerations. But it's also important to start with a big-picture approach and determine where your organization's digital challenges emerge. Your website and entire digital marketing strategy is critical to the success of your business, but you probably don't know how a key asset such as your website is underperforming. You may not know how many visitors you receive on a daily, weekly, monthly basis. Where does that traffic come from, and what do you want those individuals to do when they interact with your website?

That brings me to the objective of this book. I'm tired of watching companies do haphazard, online marketing driven by poorly-constructed and dismally-maintained websites. I'm tired of watching them spend what few marketing dollars they have on things they could either go without, or could invest in at a later date when their marketing budgets might be stronger. And I'm also tired of watching them deploy initiatives that aren't tracked using customized metrics that provide a real-time view of how a campaign is performing. The only good marketing decisions your company can make involves analysis with empirical data—otherwise you're just making random, educated guesses.

In other words, the goal of this book is to help companies of all sizes allocate their digital marketing budgets in the most effective ways possible, starting with website optimization and building out. That means focusing on three areas: the development of your brand, pleasing Google the machine and satisfying the needs and wants of your existing or prospective clients. That's it. Because as I mentioned earlier, people visiting your website want to know, they want to go, they want to interact, or they want to buy. I'm going to provide the insights and tools your team needs to develop a coherent and comprehensive marketing strategy that gives your online audience exactly what they want, when they want it.

One last point: you might notice something different about the format of this book. I'm a fan of storytelling and I tend to get bored by how-to guides. So, I've written it as a narrative in which a consultant works with a young marketer to solve her company's online marketing challenges. Rest assured that my fictional company faces many of the same challenges that yours does, so there's no need to worry about being bogged down reading some overly-theoretical case study, or about a fictional crisis that would almost certainly never impact your business. My goal is to tell a story and offer some interesting marketing insights along the way. I've even included a few personality types in my characters that you might recognize from your own office.

As you may have guessed by now, online marketing is more than my job—it's my professional passion. I hope to share the best practices that saved my business and career from recessionary ruin, all while helping to shield your marketing team from the kind of avoidable online marketing mistakes that waste budgets and get people fired.

So, let's get started.

Chapter 1

It's not every day that you get the kind of fresh start a new job can bring: a new opportunity, a chance to meet new people, and the ability to experience a whole new way of working.

I awoke on that sun-drenched Monday morning with only hope and possibility on the horizon. Sure, I'd had more than a few dead-end marketing internships since moving to New York, but this was different. This was my first real job, and I was determined to make my presence felt. DesignSpace seemed like a fun, progressive company, and the opportunity couldn't have come at a better time. I didn't know what I'd do if I had to listen one more time to my mother's lecture on why turning twenty-eight signaled my need for meaningful, career-focused employment. As if I didn't know that already—even if I wasn't quite ready to embrace the idea.

After a quick shower and a few minutes to get dressed and throw on some makeup, I looked—for about the twentieth time—at the email I'd received from DesignSpace, a company that builds office furniture and de-signs spaces, two weeks earlier.

"Congratulations, Susan," wrote Joe Cunningham, my new boss. "On behalf of our team, we'd love to welcome you aboard and offer you the marketing assistant position."

My heart was racing as I read it again—then five more times. I knew I was ready for this challenge, and I was so eager to get started.

Still, my mind was overwhelmed with negative thoughts: *You have almost no marketing experience. Your most extensive work experience involved serving lattes. How does a political science degree possibly qualify you to do this job? Sure, you have some low-level marketing experience, but is that enough? What if you get fired the first week?*

I took a deep breath and reminded myself of all the reasons I'd signed on when Joe made the offer: DesignSpace is known for its great workplace culture, Joe Cunningham is supposed to be a really nice boss, and the company scored high on the few rating websites that I bothered to check. It was going to work. It had to work.

But what if it didn't?

"You know it's 8:35, right?"

My head whipped to the side. Helen, my roommate, stood in my bedroom doorway, reminding me that all the time I'd spent preparing and fretting would have been better spent rushing to the bus and setting out to my new place of employment—about an eight-minute trip, according to the dry run I'd done on the weekend.

"Dammit!" I yelled, checking the clock on my bedside table. I grabbed my bag, stuffed in a thermal mug of carefully crafted organic coffee (I knew how to make it, after all), and headed out.

I managed to catch the 8:40 bus, and as we pulled into traffic, I took in the somber faces on the people in the seats around me. Their eyes conveyed a mix of emotions—from fatigue and stress to sheer dread. Not me. Not this time. My heart was pounding. This was a chance to shift my career into high gear.

A smile crept across my face as I pulled out my phone to browse the DesignSpace website one more time. *You never know, right? What if my day started with a pop quiz on ways to improve the site?*

I googled "DesignSpace" and found the company occupying third place on the search results page—not first. Also, the description underneath the URL had nothing to do with what DesignSpace actually does, but it was definitely the right domain.

Not for the first time since I'd applied for the position, I found myself feeling more than a little dismayed at the site's sorry state, not to mention the terrible way it displayed on a mobile device. It was completely outdated. In fact, it had barely been touched since it was built in 2005. That was surprising, because DesignSpace has a reputation for being a very progressive company. I quickly took note of how the homepage copy describing the company differed from the overview that Joe had provided during the interview process.

To make matters worse, the text was so small I could barely read it, even with some squinting. Maybe with a zoom? No, still too small. I had to read the pages section by section. "I definitely have my work cut out for me," I said under my breath. The woman in the seat next to mine gave me a strange look and edged away a couple of inches. I probably would have done the same.

Like any stereotypical millennial on a smartphone, my focus quickly shifted away from work to my Facebook app, which already had thirty-three likes on the update I'd posted before leaving my apartment: "Getting ready for a great first day," it read. My mom posted a nice, "Congratulations, honey." A little embarrassing, but it still made me smile.

The bus whizzed past the Caffeinated Bean, the coffee shop where I used to work—great memories, to be sure.

Back to my newsfeed. Why do celebrities make videos of themselves in compromising positions if they don't want anyone to see them? Ugh. Just then, a terrifying thought occurred to me. *How am I supposed to tell Joe that his website is a disaster?* What, I wondered, had I gotten myself in to?

I leaned back into the thinly padded bus seat and tried to calm my churning stomach. "I'm the right person for the job," I muttered to myself, before my seat neighbor grabbed her laptop bag and made for the door, no doubt relieved to get away from my not-so-internal voice.

I tried to reassure myself again. I know the Web. I know social media. I've got thousands of friends on Facebook, Twitter and Instagram. Joe wouldn't have hired me if he didn't think I could do the work, right … right? As we entered a busy intersection, I looked out the window and saw the building that DesignSpace called home. I pulled the cord to signal my stop, walked to the front of the bus and stepped onto the street and into a new phase of my life.

I handed my brand new ID card to the security guard in the lobby of the tower where DesignSpace resided. "Geez," I said, smiling, "it's easier to break into a bank vault than to get into this place."

The security guard was not amused. "The elevator is that way," he said, returning my badge and gesturing toward the bank of lifts to the right of his desk. I crossed my fingers and hoped that Joe would be in a better mood.

The ride to the twenty-first floor felt like the longest of my life. Sure, I'd been to the office a handful of times, but this was different. Now I was on the clock. I was being assessed and expectations were high. And I still didn't quite know what to expect.

I stepped off the elevator and took a sharp left toward the DesignSpace foyer. As with most small companies these days, there was no receptionist waiting to greet me with a smile. Just a desk piled with papers and a sign bearing the corporate logo.

Just then, a woman who looked to be in her late thirties passed through the hallway adjacent to the reception area, reading her phone intently. She didn't notice me at first, but when she did, she offered a welcoming smile.

"Susan, right?"

Roxanne is one of those employees you keep around for a lifetime. She's a hard worker, she's eager to learn and she has a knack for coming up with great ideas at ideal times. Or at least that's how Joe described her at my first interview. I think she handles inbound orders and sales. I was just happy that she greeted me by my first name—or any name, for that matter.

"Great to see you, and congratulations!" she said, holding out her hand to shake mine. "Looking forward to working with you!"

"Thanks, Roxanne, good to see you too," I replied. "I'm not really sure where I should go. Joe mentioned you were a little short on office space, so I was to meet with him to get settled in."

"No problem. We've got lots of space, but I think Joe wanted to introduce you to a couple of new people, so follow me."

Roxanne walked me over to Joe's assistant, George, who seemed overwhelmed by the many tasks assigned to him that day. Still, he managed a smile when he looked up and saw me.

"Susan, great to see you, and welcome!" he stood up from behind his desk and shook my hand.

"Thanks, George, really looking forward to it."

Roxanne turned and walked back to her desk. "Have a good morning, and if you need anything, just ask."

So far, so good. It was barely 9:30, and I'd already spoken with two new colleagues, both of whom were more than welcoming.

George sat back down and motioned to a seat opposite his desk. "Joe's tied up in an early meeting, but he should be out shortly," he said. "Have a seat."

The words were barely out of George's mouth when Joe walked in, trailed closely by a man I hadn't met before. He was older than me, maybe in his late thirties, but younger than Joe, who, as a youthful forty-three-year-old, resembled one of those Silicon Valley billionaire CEOs who dress so unassumingly you'd swear they were rank-and-file employees.

The man was wearing yellow-tinted glasses, a pair of designer jeans, high-polish wingtip shoes and a crisp white French-cuff dress shirt with no cufflinks. The shirt was pressed to ironed-cotton perfection. He looked like a well-dressed ancient rocker.

Joe stuck out his hand and I quickly reciprocated.

"Susan, I'm so glad you're here. Welcome!" he said, seeming as genuine as he had during the interview process. "I'd like to introduce you to someone. This is my old friend Dave, whom I've known for the better part of a decade now. We've been discussing how best you can help us out and become a great member of our team."

I was more than a little confused. I'd never met Dave and had no idea what his role at DesignSpace was. *Don't get flustered, don't get flustered,* I repeated in my head. I stretched out my hand to meet Dave's. He had a slightly crooked smile.

"Hi, Dave, nice to meet you," I said. What I really meant was: "Hi, Dave, who the hell are you and why does it seem like you could be my boss when that was supposed to be Joe's job?"

"You too, Susan," said Dave. "I've heard a lot about you from Joe. Don't tell him I told you, but he's really excited about having you on board." Joe gave Dave a friendly shot in the shoulder.

"You're going to ruin my rep," Joe retorted, with a this-joke-is-safe-for-the-workplace tone. With a broad grin, Joe motioned for me to follow him into the office. Dave followed close behind.

Joe had a glass-walled office with a desk at one end. Between the desk and the door were two caramel leather couches, with a coffee table in between. Joe sat on one couch, motioning to the other. Dave and I sat down.

Joe leaned forward. "My apologies for not introducing you to Dave before today, and for springing his involvement with your department on you at the last moment like this. He was traveling as we were going through the interview process, but he's done a little background research on you and agrees that you're a good fit for us."

Background research? Where? My LinkedIn page reads like an entry-level-career diary. Did he call my old manager at the Bean for a reference?

"Joe, are you trying to get your tough-boss rep back?" Dave joked, turning in my direction.

"I'm not a private investigator or anything; I just took a quick look around at some of the things you've posted online. I checked your user profiles in the different social networks, and took a general look at the face you present to the online world."

Good thing I hadn't posted those party pics from Cabo, as originally planned. I squirmed into the couch and wondered where this conversation was headed. *What, exactly, could he have noticed that made him think I was a good fit?*

He smiled. "I think you have a lot to offer DesignSpace. The fact that you have an interest in online marketing and post about it on your personal feeds is a great thing."

I'd read an article a while back that said if you want to break into an industry, you need to live and breathe it—and blogging about different industry news is one way to prove your love for the business, particularly when trying to attract the attention of a new employer. I snuck a tiny grin.

Glad to see all that effort wasn't wasted.

"Yes, but not a lot of people comment on that," I replied. "They're usually more interested in my nice beach photos."

Dave chuckled. "Sounds like Instagram," he said as he motioned back to Joe.

"Joe has asked me to walk you through what it is that *I've* learned during the last seven or eight years so that you can help Joe achieve his online marketing goals. It's different from what you've learned during your online experiences. You've got a good profile, and you haven't done anything wrong, but working on behalf of a company is different. You never know, you might even learn some new skills to carry with you for the rest of your career."

The rest of my career? Were they already planning to fire me? Unsettled, I looked to Joe, who was wearing a reassuring smile.

"Don't worry, Susan. Dave's a good guy. He'll walk you through everything he's learned so you can take all of his knowledge and apply it to make our lousy online presence better."

I could see I didn't have much choice in the matter. Best to just settle in and learn from Dave.

I turned to my new coworker – if that was what I should call him—who I now felt was more than a little annoying and tried my best sound convincing as I lied "Looking forward to working with you." My apprehension was glaring.

Joe smiled at Dave. "See?" he said. "I told you she'd be good with it."

"I asked Joe to mention my involvement before today," Dave explained shaking his head and looking at Joe, "but he thought you'd be fine meeting me on your first day. Thanks for being understanding."

"Dave's going to show you the ropes today," Joe said. "But let's get you settled first."

After a half hour of finding my desk, learning how to use the phone, getting my laptop and being introduced to the relatively small group of staff in the office, Joe asked me to follow him back into his office. Dave was perched on one of the couches, head bent over a laptop and typing quickly.

"Dave, do you want to review your role at DesignSpace?"

"Sure." He said, looking up and closing his laptop. "I'm not technically an employee of Joe's," he said, speaking directly to me, "more of a man on a mission. Joe has given me the task of turning DesignSpace's website into its best salesperson. Just don't tell Rob in sales," he added with a wink-and-nudge chuckle.

It took superhuman restraint not to groan out load. I have zero tolerance for lame office humor.

"Dave's not looking to replace anyone here, just to add a new channel—online," Joe said, visibly animated by the prospect of moving his website out of the Precambrian era.

Dave's look turned serious. "I'm not going to be your boss—that's Joe's job—but I am the one who initiated the search for the role that you eventually won."

Joe, still energized by the conversation, spoke up. "You don't have to report to Dave in any way. We'll discuss your performance during our one-on-one review meetings. But your job is to be a sponge and absorb everything you can from Dave. Dave will be reporting back to me on your overall progress, and you're both going to be accountable for our digital success. As Dave mentioned, our goal is an improved and optimized online presence, and to turn our website into our best salesperson. Sound good?"

I looked at Joe, then Dave. "Sure, looking forward to it." I'm not sure if my tone was convincing, but I was becoming increasingly intrigued by the challenge at hand.

Joe smiled. "Great. Do you two mind setting up shop somewhere else? I have a call in five."

"No problem," said Dave, packing up his laptop and standing up from the couch. "Susan, let's go hijack a conference room so we can take a look at the current online situation? I'd love to get your feedback."

"Sure," I said. "I've got my laptop now, so anywhere will do."

The butterflies quickly returned and an argument played out in my head: *I've never redesigned a website before. I'm in way over my head. I won't last a week*, said my inner pessimist.

Seconds later, my optimistic side kicked into overdrive: *You can do this. YOU CAN DO THIS! Joe seems like a good guy and he desperately needs website assistance. And it's your job. He took a chance on you and you owe him your best. Shake it off and get back in the game!*

Dave and I walked out of Joe's office, each of us shaking his hand as we went.

We made a quick detour to my new desk to drop off my bag. It was a cozy little spot with a nice welcome gift from Joe and the team—a personalized notebook and a handwritten letter from Joe explaining how excited he was to have me aboard. Not many CEOs would bother with such a personalized touch.

Soon after, Dave and I made our way to one of three empty conference rooms. The battle-scarred table and chairs looked comfortable and well-worn from many late-night planning sessions.

We took our seats at opposite sides of the table. I was a little unsure as to what to do next. I'd been expecting to deal directly with Joe, ask questions about his exact vision for the company, but no luck.

"So, you're a marketing consultant?" I asked.

"I suppose you could say that," he replied unpacking his laptop and putting it on the table. "I consider myself a digital fixer, somebody who transforms companies' online presence and helps them figure out the most efficient ways to allocate their online marketing budgets. For companies that have been operating in brick and mortar locations, I think of it as going from bricks to clicks."

Sitting across from this stranger I'd just met, I wondered if I'd been sold a false bill of goods about joining this company. I was told I'd be working with Joe, but now I seem to have been given a new boss. The early morning's excitement was quickly turning to concern, and maybe even a little bit of dread. I tried to refocus on positive thoughts. Maybe working with Dave would be a good thing. At least I hoped so.

This could be the first day of a brilliant new career, I thought, or it could be the biggest professional mistake of my young life.

Chapter 2

Dave looked at me sympathetically and spoke first.

"This whole situation probably feels a little uncomfortable," he stated. *Not at all*, I thought. *I usually start a new job only to find that a total stranger with only tenuous connections to the company is my de facto new boss. It's perfectly normal.*

"You're not sure where you stand, and that can be a little unsettling," Dave added. "I'm used to that, but usually from a different perspective." He paused to adjust his glasses. "Most of the clients I deal with are feeling exactly what you're feeling—Joe included. They understand that they have to change, and that having a great online sales channel and presence is an important part of business going forward, but they feel uncomfortable about it. That's where I come in. My goal is to give Joe an unfair advantage online. Since we're operating so far out of his comfort zone of cold calls and direct sales, he wants to be sure some of knowledge I can pass on stays in-house. That's where you come in. Make sense?"

I nodded and offered a tentative "Uh-huh."

"Would you have taken the job if you'd known you'd be working with me?"

I looked at him, not quite sure how to answer, but before I could say anything he motioned to my laptop, which was open on the conference room table. At this point, I felt as though I was back in school, being asked condescending questions by Mrs. Rahan, my seventh-grade teacher.

"Why don't we make things fair?" Dave continued. "I've done some background research on you, so now you should have the opportunity to do a little background research on me. I'll give you half an hour to poke around my website, read my blog and check out my LinkedIn profile. You should already have an invitation to connect in your inbox. While you're doing that, I'm going to take a break. I desperately need some caffeine. Would you like anything from Starbucks?"

This conversation was getting interesting. Was I going to be tested on Dave's career experience or job highlights? Who *does* this?

"Sure, a smoothie sounds great," I responded. If this job was only going to last a week or two, I might as well get a free drink out of it. (And for the record, I did *not* offer to pay for the smoothie.) "Perfect" Dave said, getting up from the chair. "I'll be back shortly. In the meantime, see what you can find out about me. I'll quiz you later." And with that little comment, he walked out of the conference room and toward the elevator door.

Well, at least my instincts about the quiz had been correct.

I quickly googled Dave and began delving into his life. I found a famous photographer with the same name before landing on the right Dave's LinkedIn profile.

The page listed the books he'd written, his many digital awards, and certifications earned over the past fifteen years in business. DesignSpace was the fourth company to which he'd provided consulting services or acted as a partner. All four were somehow tied to the marketing industry.

Just then R2-D2's digitized chime of a voice rang out—my text ringtone with a message from Helen. She wanted to know how my first day was going. (I should probably point out here that I'm kind of a sci-fi fan. Specifically, I've always been a *Star Wars* nut, which is not surprising, given that I grew up in a household with two lightsaber-wielding brothers.) *Not really sure if this job is going to be what I expected, but still willing to give it a try*, I replied. *Will text when on way home. Cocktails at Fluid tonight?*

I would definitely need a drink after this disaster, I thought. But first, back to LinkedIn. Dave the yellow-tinted consultant would be back in no time, and there was no way I wanted to fail his pop quiz.

Turns out he had also founded a consumer-behavior consultancy, an incentive company that seemed to be funded by a California-based venture-capital firm—he didn't appear to be involved with either company any longer—and a promotional company. According to his bio, Dave was now a full-time consultant, providing online marketing services to companies of all shapes and sizes. *Good for you, Dave.*

I tried to remind myself that mocking sarcasm confined to one's own head is the first sure-fire sign of insanity. Or perhaps in my case it was just pure frustration.

"Age, age, age…" I muttered, scrolling up the page before noticing his birthday. Dave was almost forty.

I read through his Twitter feed, analyzed his Facebook profile and postings, and started to notice mentions of his company here, there—pretty much everywhere. Dave seemed to be quite the well-known expert in his field. Just a few weeks earlier, for example, he had been the keynote speaker at a major marketing conference. His latest book earned rave reviews in all of the big newspapers and trade publications, and on top marketing websites. *Maybe he could be a useful mentor, after all.*

Just then Dave walked back in carrying two smoothies. I looked at the second smoothie with what must have been surprise.

"I don't actually drink coffee, much to my wife's disappointment," he explained. He apparently preferred tea. Married, too. *That's one more tidbit of info about good ol' Dave.*

As he sat down, he slid my smoothie across the table and contemplated his own beverage. He took a short sip and looked across the table in my direction.

"So? What did you find out?"

I offered a quick highlight-reel summary of his career achievements and pretended to care, emphasizing his keynote work and his past entrepreneurial successes. I even managed to force out a couple of questions about his most recent consulting endeavors. When duty calls, I can feign interest with the best of them. He sat quietly, listening, then nodded in approval.

"Good," he said. "That was a pretty solid, basic overview and really amounts to about as much research as I'd did on your background. I thought it would be only fair that you know as much about me as I know about you."

I offered a small smile, not entirely fake. And I made a mental note to double-check what I'd posted online and to be more careful about what I posted in the future.

"Okay," I said. "Where do we go from here?"

"Think about the process you just went through. You did background research on me. You learned where I've been, what I've done, and what I'm currently up to. You probably formed some opinions along the way." I smiled again. The jury was still out on my opinions.

Dave continued. "What you have to bear in mind is that this is the exact process your customers will go through when researching DesignSpace online." He paused, taking a sip of his drink. "What I want you to do now is the exact same thing that you just did with my online profiles, but do it for Joe's company." This time, the grin on my face was 100 percent genuine.

"I did that when I was interviewing for the job, and a bit more this morning, on my way here on the bus."

Dave nodded in approval.

"And, your thoughts?"

I looked back down at my laptop and navigated back to Google's search page.

"Well, the information that I could find was a little bit outdated—I think the website copyright date was 2010—and I couldn't find any social media profiles or information about the company anywhere else online. I wouldn't know DesignSpace was really a company unless I'd heard about it elsewhere and gone directly to their website."

Dave smiled at me. "And?"

I looked up at him from the computer. "Well, it was my understanding that I would be the one to help fix this particular problem."

"Problem?" Dave tilted his head as he spoke. "That's an interesting choice of words. Why would you call it a problem?"

"Well, at least online, DesignSpace appears completely out of date. In fact, I almost didn't take the interview when it was offered to me, but I'm glad I did. It wasn't until I was here that I found out how great the people are and what kind of exciting stuff is going on." Okay, that last part was a bit of overkill. The truth? I was looking forward to helping Joe get his online marketing house in order, and the people did seem really nice. But the whole Dave situation was taking some getting used to—though I was beginning to realize that there might just be a reason behind his offer to let me explore his past accomplishments, and the questions that followed. Even those yellow-tinted glasses were starting to seem a little less silly.

"I completely agree, and so does Joe," Dave answered, nodding. "One thing Joe did share with me is that you were near the top of your class, at least according to your résumé, and that you'd done a lot of external work and some co-op terms in university with an agency that helps companies get noticed online. That's why I thought you'd be a great fit for DesignSpace."

I looked at him, perplexed. "So you were in the background the whole time?"

Dave smiled again, but only partially. "He flipped me your résumé about a month ago. I was at the airport in Dallas at the time. As I mentioned, Joe has made this company succeed through the force of his own will, but he's in uncharted waters now. He's a smart guy, and knows when he's out of his depth. What he's hired me to do is make his life a bit easier and turn his current sorry excuse for a website into his highest-performing salesperson. I wanted to stay out of the hiring process because that's between you and Joe. But my job is to make sure that together we bring his brand up to speed and fix all of the problems that currently exist with his online presence."

I wasn't quite sure what to say, so I stayed quiet and let him continue.

"Look, Susan, I'm not your boss. I want to earn your trust just as I've earned Joe's. The process and systems that we are going to implement are designed to help reach those online goals, but we have to work together to make it happen. He's hired me for my knowledge, but your job is to make it all happen. I'm here to get you started, then guide you and help you along the way, but you're the one who has to do the actual work—the heavy lifting. And you'll need to draw on some of your own online marketing experience, as well."

Interesting. It looks like this role might carry more responsibility than

I'd imagined. The job advertisement was for a marketing coordinator, not a full-on digital marketing manager! This has definitely been a confusing morning. There was a long silence as I weighed my options. If this was how things were going to be, I figured I might as well go along for the ride. *What's the worst that could happen?* If this didn't work out, I'd just go back to steaming out lattes at the Bean. *Okay. Forget that. I needed to make this work. I was done scraping by on only slightly more than minimum wage.* Finally, I took a deep breath and nodded. "I'm in. So, what do we do first?"

Dave leaned back in his chair and smiled. "Good. The first thing we need to do is figure out what success looks like for Joe. He wants sales, but let's brainstorm a little bit about the tactics he can use to get noticed online."

I pulled a pen and notebook from my handbag. I've always found that a sense of responsibility can overcome nervousness or even outright fear. And now, the former was slowly beginning to overtake the latter. I felt more in control than I had all morning.

"All right," Dave started. "If you're looking for information online, like you just did, where do you go?"

"Google," I answered.

"And why is that?"

"Well," I said thoughtfully, trying not to offer an overly rudimentary answer. "There are other search engines and ways to find information online, but the information provided by Google tends to be the best, so that's where I always go. It's my default starting point for any online search."

Maybe I should have applied for a job at Google instead, I thought. I could be their top salesperson with that pitch.

Dave nodded. "Good, your thoughts align with somewhere between 70 and 80 percent of the people out there. They go to Google to find what they're looking for. The other search engines are trying to improve their performance, but they're still way behind. So, let's focus where the eyeballs are, and that's Google."

He paused for a moment, then asked, "Have you ever heard of the 80/20 rule?"

I nodded. "It means that 80 percent of your return comes from 20 percent of your effort, or something like that." The marketing manager at my first university co-op placement used to mention this rule all the time, but I hadn't paid that much attention—most of my tenure was spent running errands or making photocopies. I'd disengaged when I realized I'd been hired as a gofer. It wasn't until my next two co-op positions that I'd actually learned a bit about digital marketing.

"Exactly," he said. "So, as a general rule, you want to focus most of your efforts where they'll deliver the highest return. In this situation, the majority of traffic comes from Google, so that will be our primary focus. The other search engines are a secondary focus, and we'll only deal with them once we've maximized everything we can get from Google."

Dave looked at me, no doubt hoping for some acknowledgment of the point he was trying to make. I nodded enthusiastically.

Getting back to business, Dave motioned to my laptop. "So, let's take a look at Google's homepage. Have you ever thought about what exactly you're trying to accomplish there?" I had to think about that for a moment. "Um . . . I'm trying to find the information that I'm looking for?"

"Exactly." He nodded. "But are you always looking for the same thing? Probably not. Odds are you're often looking for different types of information. This morning when you were researching my background, how did you type in your search terms? Did you use words like *who is* or *what has* or *stories about*?"

I nodded. "Yes, that's exactly what I did."

"Good," he said. "That's called your user intent. What Google tries to do is match your user intent to the search terms you've entered, and deliver the best and most accurate search results possible for that search, or query, as it's sometimes called. This is a very important concept to understand, because if you're going to help Joe get discovered online, you have to understand what users will be looking for when they're searching for products or services like the ones DesignSpace offers."

I was jotting down notes as quickly as possible.

"Yes, I'm familiar with the term 'user intent,'" I answered. "User intent is what we talk about when discussing keyword research. In fact, I've put together lists of keywords in anticipation of this subject coming up with Joe. I've even done some research on the different types of keywords you can use if you're managing a Google Ad Words campaign, for example. I've also done some research on broad match, phrase match, exact match . . . "

Dave put up his hand like a traffic cop, halting my explanation in mid-air. "Whoa, whoa! That's all good stuff, but if it's not used properly, that type information can be as dangerous as it can be helpful."

I tried to hide my disappointment. Despite my relative lack of experience, I had actually tried to prepare for the job before my first day. And now it turned out that I had been studying the wrong trends and concepts? *Or had I?* "How so?"

"Keyword research is important, but it's not necessarily the first step. Having keywords selected is kind of like having a nail in your hand. You know its purpose and you know what it can do, but if you don't have an overall strategy and plan in place, you don't know where that nail should go. It's a part of the solution when you're building something, but it's not the whole solution. The wrong application of a keyword is like hammering a nail into the wrong place. Without a plan, you could put that nail through a piece of wood into a water pipe or electrical cable. Or what if you haven't thought through all the tools you'll need and brought a drill instead of a hammer, and you end up trying to smash the nail into the wall with the drill? It may eventually work, but it's not the best or most efficient use of either the drill or the nail."

"So, I guess this isn't hammer time, is it?" Now I was the one making terrible office jokes—and about online marketing, no less. Dave smiled but ignored my quip. He was in the zone, and in full consulting mode at this point.

"Keywords are like that," he continued. "They're good to know and essential to effective targeting, but they have their place in the process, and that place isn't first in line."

I leaned back in my chair, a little disappointed. "So, what you're telling me is I've wasted my time, and that I did all that work for nothing?"

He smiled. "No, thankfully that's not what I'm saying at all. Keyword research is very important, but it has to align with your online marketing plan. And your plan should be built on serving up an answer that gives a direct response to a specific search query. Or to put it in English, build a page that answers something people type into Google."

I was slightly confused but suddenly very intrigued.

"So, let's go back to user intent," Dave continued. "When someone is looking for a particular nugget of information, they type some keywords into Google. That's the search query. The search engine tries to determine the intent of that query in order to serve up the best results. It uses a bunch of different information and influencing factors to determine accurate and relevant results for you. Google is so confident they're going to give you the correct results, they even have an 'I'm feeling lucky' button that takes you straight to the first result."

I looked at him, raised my eyebrow, and thought for a moment. "You know, I've never actually used that button."

Dave nodded. "Most people don't. They prefer to choose, but the results they see are based on a number of factors. Google takes into account everything from the user's location to the language they've used for their search. Now, some people may type specific geographic triggers right into their search query—like New York City or Toronto—but most people don't. In those cases, the search engine has to try to anticipate the nature of the person's search. But even this can get confusing."

Tell me about it. My head was spinning and my hand was starting to cramp from all the furious note-taking.

"For example, someone searching for a restaurant may type in the words *Boston pizza*. If that person was in, say, Toronto, the results would show a number of different franchise locations for the restaurant chain called Boston Pizza. However, if someone in Boston typed in that exact same search, they would get a list of pizza joints that are in close proximity to their neighborhood. Do you see the difference?"

I nodded. "It makes sense, I guess. I just never thought about it that way."

Dave removed his yellow-tinted shades, revealing dark brown eyes that looked tired but very much alive as he dove further into what was clearly one of his favorite topics.

"Hopefully, this helps you understand why you have to take user intent into account when considering the types of keywords people could potentially use when searching for DesignSpace. When you were searching for information before your interview and before coming here today, what did you type into Google?"

"DesignSpace," I said. "That's what we would call a branded search," Dave replied. "You typed the specific name of Joe's company into Google. Did DesignSpace show up first?"

"No," I shook my head. "I think it was second or third on the list."

Dave motioned to my computer. "Now type that in again on this DesignSpace laptop."

I keyed in *DesignSpace* and there it was, top of the list.

I looked at Dave, surprised. "It's showing up first now."

I pulled out my smartphone. "It didn't show that way this morning when I searched for the company."

Dave stood up and started pacing back and forth. "You're searching for DesignSpace from the company's actual network, and because multiple people over the years have keyed in that same search from this location, on this network, even on this computer. Google takes that search history into account when serving up results. Remember, their goal is to produce the most relevant search results for each individual user, so Google knows that when people are searching for DesignSpace from this computer, this is the most relevant result."

I looked up from my phone.

"However," Dave continued, "when you were searching for DesignSpace on your phone before you worked here, Google couldn't discern your particular user intent. But that's not really Google's fault. It all comes down to the fact that the company doesn't have a strong online brand. Does that make sense?"

It did. I knew Dave was talking about custom search results. Google tries to provide the best search results it can based on your intent, previous search history, current physical location, and specific preferences once you're logged into their platform. Otherwise, it tries to use its algorithm to determine your search history based on your IP address, as well as what other users have searched in a similar situation, utilizing that implied intent methodology.

I looked at Dave. "So, what you're saying is we're going to try to manipulate the search engine so that it always shows DesignSpace when people search for it."

Dave chuckled. "No. We're not going to manipulate. The absolute last thing we are ever going to try and do is manipulate search engine results. All that does is work in the short term and then destroy your results later on, once Google figures out what you've been doing. At that point, they'll update the algorithm to eliminate you from their search results." Okay, so maybe *manipulation* was the wrong word.

"You probably weren't interested enough in online marketing to hear or care about Google's Panda, Penguin, and Hummingbird updates a while back, but what they basically did was attempt to eliminate people who had manipulated the Google search results to make sure their companies showed up first in the rankings."

Now I was confused. "But aren't we *trying* to get DesignSpace to show up first on Google?"

"Yes, that's exactly what we're doing," he said, "but we're not going to try and manipulate anything. We're just going to try and provide the best user experience and be the most helpful page for a particular user query so that Google will rank DesignSpace higher than its competitors."

"Okay, so basically what you're saying is that if we do the right thing, Google will reward us by displaying us first when people search for DesignSpace, correct?"

"Yes, that is the goal. We want to show up for people searching for DesignSpace, and for Joe's products and services. This is a really important brand exercise. I can't overstate how important . . . " Dave's voice trailed off as he caught site of the time on my laptop. "Is it noon already? I'm really sorry, but I have to run. I have an appointment across town. It looks like we'll have to wrap for now."

He started to quickly gather his things. I watched, wondering what I was supposed to do once he was gone. I didn't have to wait long for part of my answer.

"I was wondering if you wouldn't mind doing a bit of homework for me," he said.

Here it comes. I resisted the urge to roll my eyes. *I knew it. This is the part of the conversation where Dave flicks off his cool, engaging consultant switch and drops into condescending mode.*

"By the way, I'm not trying to be condescending here by sounding like a school teacher . . . "

Can he read my thoughts, too?

"But when I do seminars on this stuff, I usually prepare cheat sheets for people to take away and use as a reference. I'm going to be around to help you out for the next week or so, then I'll be available by phone or email." He dug around in the timeworn brown leather satchel that he used as a laptop bag and came up with a piece of paper. "Would you mind reviewing these notes at home while I'm still in the office?"

Homework had been one of my least favorite pastimes in high school, and not much had changed since, but I was game for anything at this point.

"Sure," I replied. Dave held out the piece of paper, and I reached across the table to take it. "Here's the first sheet. I'll have more ready tomorrow. I have to run, but I'll see you back here at nine sharp. Sound good?"

"I'll be here," I answered as Dave grabbed his bag and darted out of the room.

I carried my laptop back to my desk and spent the rest of the day working through a file that Joe had left on my desk detailing DesignSpace's many—mostly failed—attempts at online marketing over the past few years.

Around 5:30, I noticed Joe walking toward my desk with a smile.

"You should get out of here," he said. "I'm sure you're overwhelmed with all the information that Dave's been bombarding you with. Is everything working out?"

"Yep. So far, so good," I answered. What else was I supposed to say?

"Perfect, I'll see you tomorrow." Joe headed for the exit, and I logged out of my computer, packed my things, and sent Helen a text.

Still up for drinks?

Barely a minute passed when her reply sent my phone into a droidian frenzy: *On my way.*

Fluid was about a ten-minute walk from my apartment, a trendy wine and cocktail bar that attracted everyone from hipster writers—which, as I knew from my own experience interacting with aspiring scribes at the Bean, was a career synonym for *barista*—to corporate types looking to kick back at the end of a long day. For me, it was my local, and one of the few bars I felt comfortable frequenting.

I took a seat by the window, removed my coat, and noticed Helen making her way through the door. She had three shopping bags in tow.

"I know, don't say it," she said, predicting the scolding to come. "Barney's had a huge shoe sale and I just couldn't resist."

As a human resources manager at a top downtown financial company, Helen had the disposable income to shell out on really expensive clothes. The only reason we still lived together was because we were good friends—and because cheap rent meant she could channel all of her income into her shopping habit.

A waitress approached our table.

"I'll have a vodka and soda," Helen requested, before turning back to me with a beaming smile. "So, how did it go?"

I decided to unload on her.

"Okay, I think. It's a bit more responsibility than I expected and, well . . . I think it'll be okay. Maybe. Well, if it doesn't work out I'll at least learn a bit more about online marketing. It's all a lot to take in, and my sort-of boss kind of looks like an even more pretentious version of Bono and . . . you know what? Maybe I should have ordered a double."

"Well," Helen said, leaning forward as her smile broadened to a Cheshire cat–like grin. "Looks like I need more details."

Later that night when Helen and I finally made our way home, she stumbled to her room and I dug through my bag for Dave's cheat sheets.

"Better late than never," I said aloud, realizing that my alarm would sound in little more than six hours; our brief after-work drink had turned into a three-hour affair when more friends turned up unexpectedly.

Dave's notes were neat, concise, and actually very informative. I gave them a quick read before heading to bed, unsure of what the next day might bring.

Chapter 2 Takeaways

✓ Developing a strategy begins by determining what online success looks like for your organization

✓ Google is the go to search engine for 70-80 per cent of users, meaning optimizing searches for that engine is critical; other search engines are secondary in terms of priority

✓ Google's aim is to match user intent to the search terms being entered, and deliver the best and most accurate search results possible for that search, or query

✓ Keyword research should always align with an organization's online marketing plan

✓ User intent should always be taken into account when considering the types of keywords people could potentially use when searching for a company

✓ Custom search results are based on user intent, previous search history, current physical location, and specific preferences once a user has logged into their platform

Chapter 3

The next morning was a blur.

One too many cocktails the night before led to a pounding headache. Not only that, but I slept straight through my alarm; the resulting wake-up adrenaline rush propelled me out of bed and into the shower.

My head felt like it was full of cement, but I knew that a couple of extra espresso shots would help revive me so I could at least try to communicate with Dave.

I used every second of a harried half hour to my advantage. I made it out the door, to the bus, and to work on time, but with only minutes to spare. I arrived at my desk to find an email from Dave saying that he was waiting for me in the boardroom. Normally I'd have checked my account on the way into work, but all I could focus on today was TMZ's crazy headlines.

I was hoping Dave might be late, giving me extra time to get settled in for the long day ahead, but no such luck.

I took one last giant gulp from my stainless steel mug of home-brewed coffee—there'd been no time to stop for my morning fix from the

Bean—grabbed my laptop, and began reviewing Dave's notes one more time as I walked toward the boardroom.

Dave was waiting at the table, tapping contentedly on his laptop.

"Good to see you," he said, noticing me when I dropped my smartphone just steps from the boardroom door. Luckily, it was wrapped in a protective cover and survived the fall unscathed. I'd cycled through three phones in the last eighteen months. Have I mentioned I'm a bit of a klutz?

"I've been looking forward to day two," I replied, offering a half smile as I tried to collect my thoughts and the pile of items in my hand.

"Great. Then let's get right into it," he replied.

Dave stood up and walked over to a white board, red pen in hand.

"I want to continue our conversation about the way Google interprets search terms. If you remember, I mentioned that all searches have a locale filter applied to them, which is your language and location. Those items are simply extra layers of targeted information about the area where the user is located. A search like this is usually a city-based inquiry."

I began typing notes into my laptop.

"Now I want to focus on the search engine results page, or SERP. The SERP . . . " Dave paused and smiled. "That's actually kind of fun to say, isn't it?" Dave's nerdy sense of humor was coming to the fore. It was grating and endearing at the same time.

"The SERP looks a little bit different depending on what people are searching for," he continued. "The information that is provided about any particular subject will be influenced by the user's country of origin and the order in which they search for information. The results in Toronto may be very different from the results in New York, for example."

He paused for a few seconds that felt like minutes. I wondered if he was seeking recognition that I understood the information, or just wanted to make sure I was wide-awake and listening. I nodded confidently. This seemed like a pretty simple concept. Dave, still standing, motioned back to my laptop and the search page filling the screen.

"Why don't you google DesignSpace," he asked. I did, and was immediately presented with 4.5 million search results.

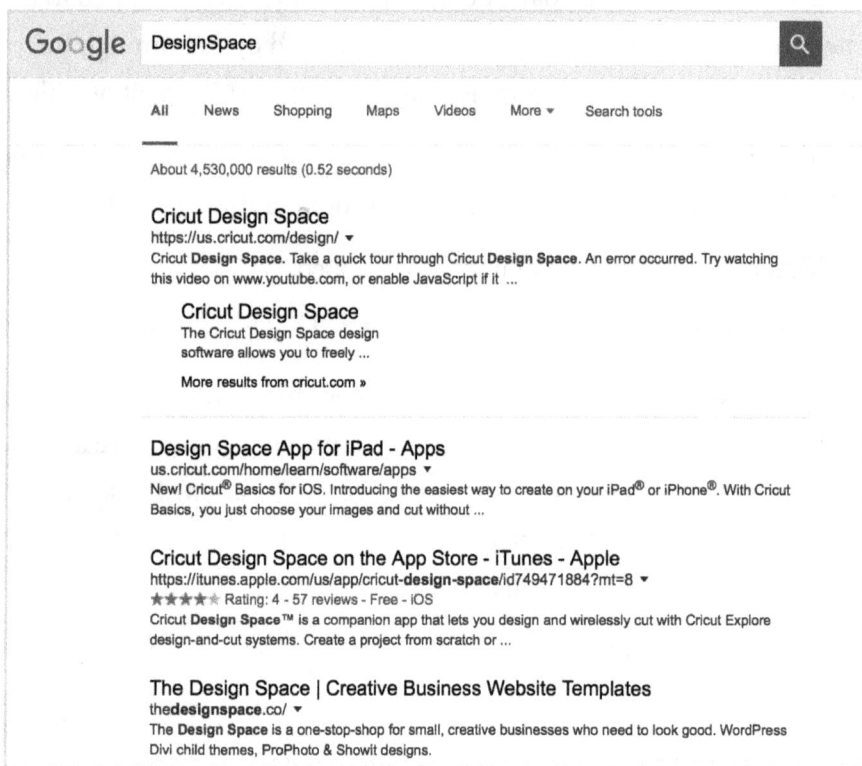

"When you look at the results you see on the page, can you tell which result Google thinks you were looking for?"

"It seems to think I was looking for an app" But that doesn't make sense. *Why would it show an app first?*

Dave looked at the screen then walked back to his side of the table.

"Yes, that's the most relevant result right now."

As Dave sat down and leaned back in his chair, I felt yesterday's confusion setting in again.

"The thing you have to bear in mind," he carried on, "is that Google wants you to click—ideally on their paid results. Barring that outcome, they want you to click somewhere, anywhere, on the page. By doing so, you're telling them they were successful in serving you the right results for your search."

I looked up from my screen. "There's actually a lot of information to click on."

Dave nodded. "Yes, and Google tries to give you a little bit of information about each result so you can make a decision, which is where the little blocks of text about each search result come in. They're usually made up of three different things: a title, a URL, and a snippet."

The Design Space | Creative Business Website Templates
thedesignspace.co/ ▾
The **Design Space** is a one-stop-shop for small, creative businesses who need to look good. WordPress Divi child themes, ProPhoto & Showit designs.

I focused back on my screen as Dave continued, scanning the results on the page.

"The title is a short description of what the website is about; if it's a branded search the title would normally be the name of the company. So when you searched for DesignSpace, that should show at the top." "Yep," I confirmed.

"Good," he said. "Underneath that you should see a website address and a snippet of information about that website."

I leaned in to get a better view of the screen. "It's got the URL, but the snippet— that little description underneath—is a bit strange. It's not written very well, or in proper English, for that matter." I chuckled and grabbed my pen.

"I guess this is one of the things on my to-do list," I said.

Dave smiled. "Absolutely. And by the way, there's a great app called Evernote that helps you do what you're doing on your notepad, but syncs it across all your devices."

I looked up at him from my notebook. "I've heard of that, but didn't know exactly what it was."

He motioned to my notebook. "It's cool. You can even snap photos of your notes from your notebook, and it'll recognize your handwriting. You can also search in Evernote for particular words, and the app will highlight specific words in that photo of your notes. There are a lot of note-taking apps out there. Evernote is just one of them."

Somewhat ironically, I made a note in my book to download the app. I admit I appreciated Dave's tip. Yesterday, I might have considered it condescending, but I was beginning to realize that he really did take pride in helping DesignSpace achieve success. *I think he was pulling for me, too.* "Let's get back to the DesignSpace website," he said, pulling up a chair so he could see my laptop with clarity. "Now, click on the title link or the URL. What happens?"

I did as he asked and examined the results on my screen. "It takes me through to the DesignSpace homepage, which needs some work." I laughed. "Also on my to-do list, right?"

"You're absolutely correct," he smiled again. "But what I wanted you to notice here is the page you were taken to. It's called the landing page. The landing page is often the homepage of a website, but it doesn't have to be. The landing page experience is the most important thing that Google uses to determine the relevance of its results."

I nodded, and this time I was confident that I understood Dave's point. "I think I know where you're going with this. Google takes a user's search terms, analyzes them, and tries to offer up the most relevant results, hoping that people will click on the first couple of results because they're the most relevant for their search. Those results could be advertisements, organic, or even local results." "You've got it," he said, a broad smile crossing his face. "Do you want to take a second to get another coffee? You looked a little tired when you walked in this morning." My face turned beet red. Was it that obvious that I'd slept in and had to rush to work? I thought I'd done a pretty good job of pulling myself together, especially considering I'd only had a half hour to get ready.

"I was up late reviewing your notes," I answered cleverly. "But I'm good. No need for more caffeine just yet."

Dave grinned. "Well, at least your late night was productive." He clearly knew that my night had involved more than a simple review of his notes, and probably a few cocktails too many.

Maybe that's why he reached into his bag and pulled out a sheet with more notes to review.

"I know I'm bombarding you with new terms and information, so here's another cheat sheet to read when you have a minute. You'll probably forget some of these terms over the next day or two. Even I have a tough time remembering all of this stuff."

I knew that wasn't true, but I appreciated his efforts to seem relatable.

Cheat Sheet – Definitions

User intent: When a user types a query, he or she is trying to accomplish something. We refer to this goal as the user intent.

Locale: All queries have a locale, which is the language and location for the task.

User location: Some queries also have a user location, which provides more specific information about where the user is located. The user location is usually a city.

Search engine results page (SERP): The page a search engine shows after a user enters a query in the search box. The SERP is composed of result blocks.

SERP components: title, URL, snippet

The Landing page: The page you see after you click the title link in the result block. We use the word result to refer to the result block and the landing page.

Dave took a sip from his cup. "I really don't know how I'd be able to function without my morning tea," he commented, relaxing back into his chair again. "Do me a favor. Go to Google's search page and type in *Starbucks*."

As I was typing it in I wondered how much Starbucks invests in online marketing each year. I'm sure it's a lot more than DesignSpace. Like a million times more.

"So, what are the results?"

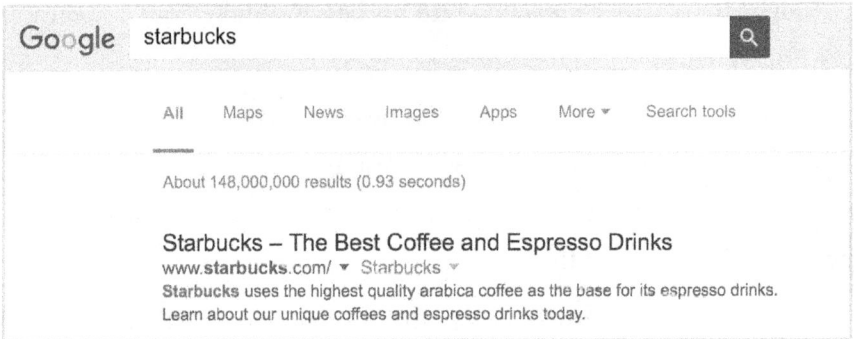

"Well, there appears to be some ads, and then below them there are links through to the Starbucks website. On the right side there's a map showing some local Starbucks locations, and below that are links to their Twitter and Facebook pages."

Dave nodded and took another sip. "But when you typed in DesignSpace, you didn't get the company as the first result, or see any ads about DesignSpace, or multiple other links to the website or social media profiles, correct?"

"No," I replied.

"This is the difference between a good online presence with lots of brand support, and one that needs some work. I'm just trying to walk you through what you should be looking for, and then what you should be striving for, as you build DesignSpace's online presence, starting with their website."

"Okay, but DesignSpace isn't Starbucks," I said, shooting a skeptical look in Dave's direction.

"Agreed, but if someone is looking for DesignSpace's products, shouldn't this company at least *appear* to have as strong a presence as Starbucks? Maybe not the multi-location element, but definitely the positive reinforcement that this is a real, established business and that the website is worth not only visiting, but exploring at length."

"I get it," I said. "You're saying that no matter the size of the company, it should still have a pretty robust online presence. But what about the fact that Starbucks has a marketing budget about a million times the size of ours?"

Dave explained that digital marketing success isn't simply the result of how much money a company has to spend. Even micro-businesses with relatively tiny budgets have been able to turn their websites into their best salespeople by using the right tactics and by building them out with great content.

"Now," he said, gesturing at my laptop, "type in *Starbucks smoothies*. What do you see this time?"

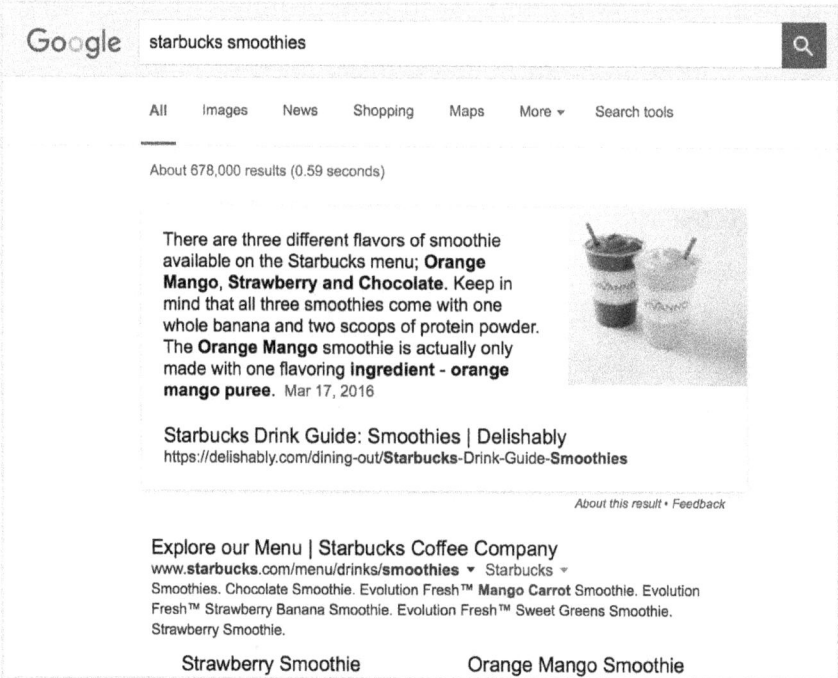

Google   starbucks smoothies

All   Images   News   Shopping   Maps   More ▾   Search tools

About 678,000 results (0.59 seconds)

There are three different flavors of smoothie available on the Starbucks menu; **Orange Mango, Strawberry and Chocolate**. Keep in mind that all three smoothies come with one whole banana and two scoops of protein powder. The **Orange Mango** smoothie is actually only made with one flavoring **ingredient - orange mango puree**. Mar 17, 2016

Starbucks Drink Guide: Smoothies | Delishably
https://delishably.com/dining-out/**Starbucks**-Drink-Guide-**Smoothies**

About this result • Feedback

Explore our Menu | Starbucks Coffee Company
www.**starbucks**.com/menu/drinks/**smoothies** ▾ Starbucks ▾
Smoothies. Chocolate Smoothie. Evolution Fresh™ **Mango Carrot** Smoothie. Evolution Fresh™ Strawberry Banana Smoothie. Evolution Fresh™ Sweet Greens Smoothie. Strawberry Smoothie.

Strawberry Smoothie   Orange Mango Smoothie

I looked carefully at the screen, attempting to apply my new knowledge. "The results page is different. There's still an ad for Starbucks at the top, but now the main result is menu-based. It looks as if the link is pointing right through to the smoothies page. And there are a whole bunch of images for Starbucks smoothies—hey, I didn't know they had orange mango."

"You learn something new every day," Dave replied. "Do you see how Google tries to serve up the most relevant result for the user? If you typed in *Starbucks smoothies* and they showed only the homepage, do you think that would be as relevant a result? Or do you think being directed right to the smoothies category page is a better result?"

I paused. *This seemed like one of those questions so rudimentary that it must deserve some sort of clever, counterintuitive answer. But I decided to play it safe.* "Um . . . getting to the right page is obviously the better result."

"Exactly," he said. "But that's all determined by the landing page that Starbucks has built for their smoothies." Just then, I noticed Joe out of the corner of my eye. He was leaning against the boardroom doorway. "Don't let me interrupt. Finish your thought, Dave."

Dave continued. "The key here is that Starbucks built a page that's both specific and addresses a specific user's intent. This enables the machine that is the backbone of Google to match up your search query with a product page associated with Starbucks. Optimization—specifically, search engine optimization, or SEO—is as simple as that. All you have to do is figure out what the user intent is, and then provide a unique landing page experience that's helpful, trustworthy, and addresses the specific user intent based on their Google search."

"Looks like you're deep into the world of online marketing, and all before 10 a.m.," Joe said with a smile. "I need you both for a quick meeting in my office."

What could this be about, I wondered as we stood up. Maybe Joe was having second thoughts about this whole marketing thing—or, for that matter, employing me as his marketing point person. I grabbed my laptop and tried to conjure positive thoughts before following Dave out of the boardroom. *No need to fear for my job just yet,* I tried to reassure myself. Joe led the way, trading pleasantries with a few DesignSpace staffers as we walked through the office. I barely knew anyone, so most of my greetings were limited to a smile and a head nod.

We arrived at Joe's office and were met by a shortish man around Dave's age, wearing a crisp white shirt, black trousers, and a pair of oxfords so highly polished I was sure I'd be able to see my reflection if I looked close enough. I didn't, choosing instead to sit down at the meeting table.

The man stood up and held out his hand. "I'm Raj," he said.

Raj Khanna was Joe's chief financial officer. He was responsible for monitoring and managing financials for all of Joe's companies. Although he offered a smile along with his outstretched hand, there was something in his expression that suggested he wasn't very pleased. Joe shut the door behind us. "Raj, Susan is working with Dave to transform our website into a sales driver. Raj is going to review a few financial details with us today. He and I do this in quarterly meetings, one of which was today. Susan, I know this might be a bit overwhelming, seeing as you've just started, but it's important for you to have a clear picture of both the opportunities and challenges we face in the months ahead."

"Good to meet you, Susan," Raj said. His stare was intense and deliberate, as if he was issuing a challenge for me to bring my A-game to the table. I used to get similar looks from customers needing their morning caffeine fix in a hurry—even when the Bean had a lineup of people that stretched out the door.

"Raj, why don't you get started," Joe said as he took a seat at the table.

Raj hooked a cable into his laptop and a PowerPoint presentation instantly appeared on the monitor mounted to the wall.

"We have a bit of a problem," he started. "The graph in this first slide shows our drop in revenue over the past six months. Now, the economy has been a bit sluggish, but I believe much of the downward pressure on our financial performance is due to a few fundamental flaws in the way we approach the marketplace."

"What Raj is trying to say," Joe interjected, "is that our marketing strategy has been a mess for a long time." I respect a boss who's honest— and that was a pretty honest assessment.

"John—he was your predecessor, Susan—was a great guy, and he had a solid understanding of what I like to call old-school marketing, but the digital stuff was way over his head," Joe explained. He'd not been so open during our meetings. Mind you it was my second day, so it's proof that you should never judge a book by its cover. I'd assumed Joe was pretty meek, mild and, well, kind of soft. Maybe I was wrong. *Reminder to self: never judge a book by its cover.*

"I figure John cost us at least a million dollars in sales each of the five years he was here," Joe continued. "I fired him because I had to, at least if we were going to survive in a digital environment." Yep. My initial impression of Joe had definitely been off base.

"I'm not an online marketing expert, but I do know that John made a classic mistake. He assumed that because he redesigned our website and made it look prettier—although I think it could still be improved—it would essentially sell itself and ensure that we'd get noticed online. Raj, can you turn to the appendix you showed me earlier?"

Raj clicked through the PowerPoint deck until he came to a page full of statistics, almost all of them highlighted in red.

"These figures show trends in searchability for DesignSpace. As you can see, we've been down in every category for the past four years. I clearly didn't act quickly enough to make changes in the marketing department, and it hurt us—badly. Dave helped put these figures together, so he's very well acquainted with them. Susan, I want you to study these and understand that we need to make some major changes if we're going to turn this ship around."

I stared at the screen and nodded.

"Poor online searchability has definitely cost the company," Raj said. "Our revenue is down 11 percent year-over-year, while profits are down 22 percent. The way I see it, we have strong products, and our customer satisfaction rating is sky high. We should be *growing* at this point, not bleeding money, which is exactly what's happening right now."

Raj and I locked eyes for a few very uncomfortable seconds. There was that stare again. I felt as though I was being challenged to come up with a solution to what seemed like a very big problem. *But I'd only just started yesterday!*

"Look, I could go on, but I'm not sure it's necessary. It's clear that something does, indeed, have to change if DesignSpace is going to have a future," Raj stated grimly.

"Raj is right," Joe confirmed, as if that was even necessary. "And as I just explained, I think the source of many of our problems has been the marketing department. The good news, Susan, is that I think you're the best person to help us right the ship."

What was with all the nautical references?

I quickly assessed the situation in my head. *So, let me get this straight. THE ENTIRE FUTURE OF THE COMPANY is basically riding on my ill-trained, underconfident shoulders? Did Joe actually read my résumé before hiring me, or was I the only warm body left standing once the interview process played out?*

I tried to refocus as the three wise men volleyed ideas across the table.

"I hear what you're saying about buttressing our marketing operations," Raj said to Joe, "but I think what we really need to do is hire better sales staff. No offense to our marketers at the table, but I've almost never seen any kind of quantifiable return on investment delivered by a marketing initiative at any company where I've worked—including this one."

"That's probably because none of them did it right," Dave shot back. They locked eyes like two silverback gorillas getting ready to square off. I sat up a little straighter in my seat. This had the potential to get *really* interesting.

"Maybe, but if I were a gambler, I'd bet it was because they had nothing strategically viable to offer." Raj's tone was remarkably passive aggressive, but Dave was having none of it.

"I've seen a lot of marketing initiatives fail as well," Dave conceded. "But that's because they weren't developed with any clear strategy in mind to address a particular customer intent. Our plan is different. We're going to be using the latest in analytics and content development, and doing some back-end work to optimize this website and turn it into a selling tool. I guarantee you will see results. Now, do we need to complement that work with other marketing initiatives—maybe some PR or direct sales support? Absolutely. And we also have to be very strategic with budget allocation. But we have to be careful not to discount the value of the digital project Susan is working on."

"Fair enough," Raj stated, although he was still locking eyes with Dave.

"Well, it seems like we're all on the same page," Joe concluded cheerily.

If this was a consensus, I'd hate to see a full-blown argument between these guys. They seemed to barely tolerate each other.

"I'll let you and Susan get back to work," Joe said to Dave. "And you do have your work cut out for you. Let's meet again in a few days, after you've continued briefing Susan on your strategy for the website. I'll be curious to hear her thoughts on the plan."

"Sounds good to me," Dave replied, before turning in my direction. "You OK with that?"

"Uh, yep. That works for me," I answered. Let's face it: at this point, I was more fascinated by what seemed to be a clash of digital marketing philosophies—not to mention personalities—than by any website strategy!

We stood up and left Joe's office together.

"Raj is a great guy," Dave said with a smile as we walked back toward the boardroom.

Was I hearing this right? Had these guys not been ready to tear each other to pieces mere seconds ago?

"It looked like you two might not be the . . . um . . . best of friends," I replied sheepishly. Dave chuckled. "Raj and I have been friends for a long time. We went to university together. That's just our way of communicating; always has been. We really enjoy a good debate and will sometimes goad each other into a heated discussion, even when we're both pretty much in agreement on an issue. It's our way of having fun and letting off steam. We've worked in a couple of companies together where Raj has held a finance role and I've worked on the digital marketing side."

So, these guys call arguing fun? What have I gotten myself into with this job?

"Are all CFOs so against marketing?" I asked.

"No," Dave replied. "Quite the opposite, in fact. It's just that most of the time, they see marketing as a black hole for revenue. The money goes in, but it almost never comes back out. And everyone else in the company tells them that marketing needs to happen, so they should just learn to live with its unquantifiable characteristics as some inevitable fact of life. Kind of like a leap of faith. Cross your fingers and hope it works."

"That seems like a recipe for confrontation and stress. But what if they have a point?" I asked.

"They do," Dave replied after pausing for a moment. "It's our job to not only make a case for all the great things we want to do on the marketing front, but also to quantify our results. The great news is that, at least when it comes to online marketing, it's possible to do exactly that. Back in the old days, if you got coverage in a newspaper, for example, you had to rely on the paper's circulation figures and do a really complicated calculation based on the section in which the coverage appeared—its length, tone, you name it—to determine the value. Then along came the Web and most of these issues disappeared over time. Now we measure success in clicks, user engagement, social media shares, and a whole host of other relevant metrics. It's really quite fascinating how fast things move nowadays, especially when it comes to digital marketing. I've got to admit, that's not always a good thing." That was news to me. I thought this whole rapid pace of change in the marketing world was some kind of wonderful revolution—a sign of progress that we should embrace.

"That's bad?" I asked.

"It is, because if you don't alter your digital marketing strategy on an ongoing basis, you're setting your organization up for almost certain failure. DesignSpace is the perfect example. They had a person running their website and other online marketing initiatives, but he wasn't particularly good at his job. Joe didn't push for changes because he doesn't understand this stuff as well as he should—which he's the first to admit—and it's come back to bite him."

"So, what you're saying is we're pretty much screwed thanks to the near-insurmountable challenge ahead?" I wondered rather bluntly.

Dave laughed out loud.

"No," he answered, trying to hold back another belly laugh. "I think we just have a lot of work to do. You ready to dive back in?"

"Sure, let's do it."

✓ When reviewing a SERP, remember that information that is provided about any particular subject will be influenced by the user's country of origin and the order in which they search for information

✓ Search engine website descriptions, or the result block, usually consist of a title, a URL, and a snippet

✓ The landing page, often the home page of a website (but not always), is the most important thing that Google uses to determine the relevance of its results

✓ A strong online presence with adequate brand support should mean that your company displays at the top of search engine rankings for your company name or industry, and should generate multiple inbound links to your website. That includes extensive traffic to your company's social media accounts

✓ The key to SEO is determining user intent, then providing a unique landing page experience that's helpful, trustworthy, and addresses the specific user intent based on their Google search

✓ Online marketing strategies should be revised regularly to remain relevant and deliver maximum impact for your organization

Chapter 4

"I should start by explaining something about Google," Dave continued, picking up our earlier conversation as if the meeting with Joe hadn't happened.

"Google is a for-profit company. They make their money by selling ads. They want these ads to be seen and clicked on by people who are using their search engine. However, the only way they can keep people coming back to their search engine is by providing the most relevant, helpful, and trustworthy results possible. So, when you're designing any page, ask yourself these questions: Is this page relevant? Is this page helpful? Is this page trustworthy? If your page is the most helpful, the most relevant, and the most trustworthy, Google will show it first. It's as simple as that."

I knew there had to be a catch. There's no way any company can log revenue in the tens of billions of dollars each year without having some kind of highly complicated tricks up its sleeve.

"But what about the ads at the top?" I asked.

"The good news is that those ads must follow the same rules, but there's a bit more flexibility if somebody is willing to bid enough money. The reason why unpaid, organic search engine results pages are clicked on much more frequently than ad pages results is because people trust the unpaid results more than they trust the paid results. People are smart. They realize companies are paying to be at the top of the search engine results page, and they conclude that if those companies really were that good, Google would show them organically."

"That makes sense when you really think about it," I said. "I hardly ever click on the ads."

"You're not alone," Dave agreed, "but millions of people do, each and every day. Google's ad auction works by awarding the ads to pages that are the most relevant, the most helpful, and the most trustworthy; they do this through something called a *quality score*. We'll get into that later, but basically what it means is the more relevant, trustworthy, and accurate the results are for the keywords you've chosen as part of your Google Ad-Words campaign, the less money you have to pay for those particular keywords." I'd been following along just fine up until that last part, but now I was getting confused. Dave must have recognized my mild befuddlement.

"Let's not confuse things or get ahead of ourselves," he said with a smile. "For now, let's just talk about how to get DesignSpace's website noticed organically in the regular search engine results. From a strategic perspective, we have to show Google that DesignSpace's site is the dominant interpretation of any search for the company, and is the official webpage associated with DesignSpace. Lets start with the understanding that every company has its own brand. Right now, DesignSpace has its own brand, but it isn't being recognized online. We have to fix that." He reached into his messenger bag, which was sitting under the table.

"Here you go. More notes so you can recall some of these terms easily, as well as a few extra terms that you should know." I had to admit that I was really beginning to appreciate the cheat sheets. I was familiar with some of these concepts, but having notes for reference was a big help.

The Vital (V) rating is used for Title Link Result Blocks (TLRBs) in these very special situations:

• There is a dominant interpretation and clear user intent to navigate to a specific website or webpage, and the landing page of the TLRB is exactly what the user is looking for.

• The dominant interpretation of the query is an entity (such as a person, place, business, restaurant, product, company, organization, etc.), and the landing page of the TLRB is the official webpage associated with that entity.

Dave stood up and started to pace back and forth across the boardroom. When I glanced up from the page, he started speaking again.

"We have to set up DesignSpace's homepage with a particular objective in mind, so Google understands it's the "vital" search result for that objective, and should be shown first." he said. "The first thing we want to do is make sure Google recognizes, both from a machine perspective and from a user perspective, that this is the most relevant result for that particular search for this company. One of the ways we can do that is by looking at the search query from a utility perspective. DesignSpace's homepage, therefore, should be the most relevant result that matches the specific user intent of people searching for DesignSpace. The goal is to produce a relevant, topical, helpful, and high-quality result. Does that make any sense?"

"Well, yes, but isn't it really obvious that DesignSpace should be the first result that appears for people searching for a company in New York called DesignSpace?" I looked at Dave, waiting for some kind of counterintuitive revelation to be thrown my way, but not this time.

"You're exactly right," Dave confirmed, much to my satisfaction. "And that's what a lot of people fail to realize: search engine optimization is a very logic-driven process. There aren't really any tricks or surprises involved. In fact, Google wants to avoid any attempts to manipulate search engine results, which is why they'll readily blacklist companies or individuals they suspect of trying to game their system. And believe me, if you're running a business, you really don't want to be blacklisted by the biggest and most influential search engine on the planet."

"So, no cheating, then?" I asked with a grin.

"Nope, definitely no cheating," he answered. "But on your to-do list you'll need to pay special attention to key considerations such as title tags, meta-descriptions, header tags, and meta-keywords. If you turn over the page I just gave you, you'll see a few more definitions."

Cheat Sheet – Online Search Definitions

Title tags are the top line that shows in the title of the search engine results page.

Meta-descriptions are the snippet that shows underneath the URL.

Meta-keywords tell the machine what the page is about. Meta-keywords should only be four or five words in length, maximum

"The thing about meta-keywords is that the Google machine is usually pretty good about determining from the text on the page what that particular page is about. However, it doesn't hurt to reaffirm that fact by using header tags, which are simply bolded tags used along with the text on your site to help reinforce what the page is about. Then there's content to consider."

"Wait," I paused for a moment to collect my thoughts. "Haven't we been talking about content?"

"Not really," Dave answered. "Nowadays, search engines like Google place a huge emphasis on the quality of the content on your website. That includes everything from the text or copy on your various web pages to the site's relevance to your target audience, as I mentioned earlier. It even includes the frequency at which you're making updates. That's why it's so important to have a blog or some other element on the website that can be updated regularly. Video is another very search-friendly element. And we can't forget a well-maintained social media presence. That's a crucial element too. We'll discuss that in more detail later if we have time."

I was writing notes as quickly as possible. "Got it," I said.

"Let's just say that having a 'fresh' set of web pages indicates to Google that your website is well maintained, even though the best-performing results might be ones that are archived, or even older."

Dave reiterated that Google's ultimate goal is to identify user intent. "As an example, let's take somebody who is online in Kansas in the middle of tornado season and is looking for some breaking news on a twister that just touched down somewhere near their town. Google will try to serve the most relevant results to that person based on their location and the information they're currently searching for. It wouldn't be helpful for that person to be served a list of the top ten most destructive tornadoes of all time if they're concerned about a tornado bearing down on them right now, would it?"

"Definitely not."

"The same thing happens with global events like the FIFA World Cup or the Olympics. People who are searching for a particular soccer player would want the most recent results from the global tournament currently being played, as opposed to specific information about somebody else by that same name."

Dave was on a roll. Clearly, he was particularly passionate about this whole search thing. Although I really like working in marketing, I don't think I'll ever be able to work up any kind of legitimate enthusiasm for an algorithm that finds websites online. *To each their own, I suppose.*

"Other types of information people might be looking for include statistics—maybe the population of Paris, the amount of U.S. debt at the current interest rate, or airfare from Toronto to New York," Dave went on. "This is current and fresh information, and Google will attempt to display the most relevant results. For people looking for a particular product, any kind of registered trademark or brand-based query is usually the top result. If you Google the word *Coke*, for example, you should be directed to the website of the Coca-Cola Company. Again, it comes down to trustworthiness, user-friendliness, and relevancy."

"That's funny. I thought it might show a picture of this jittery, overly hyper stockbroker named Randy who used to come into the Bean every morning," I said with a laugh.

"Right, so let's keep moving," Dave replied, completely ignoring my only somewhat inappropriate narcotics reference. I could feel my face morphing—at warp speed—from white to pink to red.

"Ahem." I cleared my throat, desperately trying to steer the conversation away from my apparently ill-timed remark (although I still thought it was pretty funny). "I've been thinking about it, and I really feel we should include a blog component as part of the regular updates to the site. Do you think that would be beneficial?"

"Absolutely. As I mentioned earlier, having fresh content is really important for improving and maintaining healthy search engine rankings. Our goal is to be the most on-topic, helpful, and high-quality result that shows in the Google search engine page. That means choosing blog topics that make sense for our target clientele, and offering information that provides real value to those readers. Having highly relevant blog posts and information about what the company is up to, industry developments, new products and services, and even thought leadership content is great for Google. All of that information helps the search engine determine that we're the most formidable authority on this particular subject."

"Thought leadership?" I asked,

"Yep," Dave replied. "That could be Joe writing about industry news or offering tips to DesignSpace's clients. You know, kind of like the posts you read on LinkedIn all the time. You're familiar with that content, right?"

"Um, yep, you bet." While I had seen those posts and even skimmed a few, I have to say that reading some CEO's take on how to engage millennials wasn't usually at the top of my reading list. I wasn't about to confess that to Dave, though.

"That's why it's important to never forget the end user when preparing this type of content. Never write a blog, or even website copy, that's only designed to please the Google bot—that's the software Google uses to scour websites and determine their rankings. Write this stuff as though a person is actually going to read it and use the information provided to make a good decision. That's the kind of behavior that will eventually get rewarded with a high search engine ranking. An attempt to manipulate the Google machine won't get you there. You could say that freshness applies to products and services, as well. Nothing is static, and even something as iconic as the iPhone, which is now in its seventh or eighth generation, will see its search engine results change from one month to the next. A new iPhone release means its rankings will generally spike because that's what people want to know about at that particular time."

"Got it," I said.

"Perfect," he replied. "Now, let me ask you a question. If you went to a search engine and typed in a particular keyword and got something that had nothing to do with the subject you were interested in, would you call that a good user experience?"

I shook my head. This time I knew the answer Dave was looking for was completely straightforward. "Of course not."

Dave smiled. "Joe said you were bright. You're absolutely correct. The next consideration is trustworthiness. What does it really mean?"

"Well, I guess it means that Google is trying to make sure users don't get misled by companies that are trying to game the system, like you said before, maybe by playing tricks that fool a search engine's bots."

Dave looked pleased with my assumption. "The good thing about Google," he said, "is that it has the power of millions of bots that are constantly searching the net to find the most highly relevant search results possible for all kinds of different subjects." But as Dave went on to explain, this can be both a pro and con. Bots use indicators on webpages as important signposts to help them clarify and analyze information. As he noted, however, a butterfly can be classified as a butterfly without offering any information about the colors of the wings or the beauty and symmetry of the insect. Those are characteristics unique to each individual butterfly. If you were interested in monarch butterflies, for example, you would want information regarding that particular subspecies.

"The challenge is that people who are trying to manipulate Google the machine are well aware of the many criteria and factors that it uses in searches. So, they use those factors to try to show up first in the search engine results page to get traffic and visitors to their website. Of course, there's nothing wrong with trying to make money online, and there's nothing wrong with having ads on those SERPs to make additional money—in addition to affiliate revenue or from ads that are relevant to your users. But this means that the results the Google algorithm produces may have been manipulated by these webmasters—and that's not the result Google wants to present.

"Fortunately, over time people have noticed this kind of manipulation and have responded to it by setting up very helpful and useful websites—such as Yelp and TripAdvisor, and by commenting on Google+ pages. The goal is to try to equate the actual user experience with the information the website is presenting about itself."

"So, these websites police the unethical players?" I asked.

"You could look at it that way," Dave replied. "That said, you'll notice that just about every website has a self-promotional element. This is the kind of information the search engine web crawlers have to take with a grain of salt. That means the web bots will place a greater trust ranking on third-party reviews than the information on the website itself. This makes factors such as a strong Better Business Bureau even more important than ever."

"So, if we were talking about a hotel, a bot would place greater value on a TripAdvisor review than on a testimonial on the hotel's website?" I guessed.

"Exactly. When the website says one thing about itself, but reputable external sources disagree with what the website says, Google will use the external sources when determining where the website should rank on the search engine results page."

"Okay, so I understand, what you're saying is that there are actually two layers of trustworthiness at play here—the trust you get when you tell the machine what your website is about, and the trust you get from individual users when they're use your website, read it, or comment about it on other sites. Is that correct?"

Dave nodded emphatically. "You're absolutely right again, and that's a great way to think about it. You have to do all the right things on your website to make sure that you're found in the search engine results page from a Google 'the machine' perspective. But then, assuming that every single website in your particular customer or competitor base has done all of those same things, Google will take ratings from third-party sources to establish where you should rank on the search engine results page. It's Google that decides whether you should rank first or 101st, depending on the trustworthiness of your page and your overall online reputation."

I thought about it for a moment, then asked Dave how we could generate enough third-party reviews to get ranked higher by Google?

"There are a bunch of different places where this information is found online," Dave responded. "It could be in website reviews, references from websites such as Wikipedia, recommendations by industry experts, news articles, and other information that's written or created by individuals about your particular website and company."

"But wouldn't it take a long time to build up enough reviews to boost your rankings?" I was beginning to worry that producing results for DesignSpace could be a never-ending, uphill struggle.

"Not really," Dave reassured me. "Again, a number of factors determine a company's search rankings, not only reviews. Let's take retail stores as just one example. They frequently have user ratings not only for the particular products they sell, but also for the in-store experience. These ratings can help customers better understand that particular website's overall reputation. The larger the number of positive user reviews, the greater the evidence of a positive reputation."

I understood what Dave was saying, but I still wasn't completely sure about the workload I was facing in the months ahead.

A coy smile suddenly stretched across Dave's face. "So, what's Joe's reputation like on the Internet?"

I hesitated for a second. "To be honest, I couldn't find much information about Joe online at all. His bio on the DesignSpace website is very limited, and his LinkedIn page hasn't been updated in a really long time."

Dave nodded. He explained how common it was for small business owners to have a minimal profile online. "Let's go over some potential sources of reputational information, and then I'll review different methods you can use to conduct reputational research." The most common places to search for this kind of information, he said, are news articles, Wikipedia articles, blog posts, magazine articles, forum discussions, and ratings from independent organizations. "What you should definitely be on the lookout for are negative reputation indicators—things like credible and convincing reports of fraud or financial wrongdoing, which would be an extreme negative indicator for a website. Keep in mind that small transgressions, such as interacting with a clerk who was having a bad day, or one particular negative customer experience, should not be an overall negative indicator for the website."

Dave sat back down in front of his laptop. "I have to stop killing forests by giving you these paper cheat sheets," he said. "Let me email these notes to you. These are some specific strategies on how to search for negative reputation information. Google is, of course, the best place to start. If something is indexed on Google, that means it's impacting overall search results.

Dave clicked away on his keyboard, and within seconds my inbox chimed.

Cheat Sheet – Tactics To Search for Negative Reputation Information

1. **Identify the "homepage" of the website.** For example, for the IBM website, ibm.com is the homepage.

2. **Using ibm.com as an example, try one or more of the following searches on Google:**

    [ibm –site:ibm.com]: A search for IBM that excludes pages on ibm.com

    ["ibm.com" –site:ibm.com]: A search for "ibm.com" that excludes pages on ibm.com

    [ibm reviews –site:ibm.com] A search for reviews of IBM that excludes pages on ibm.com

    ["ibm.com" reviews –site:ibm.com]: A search for reviews of "ibm. com" which excludes pages on ibm.com

3. **Look for articles, reviews, forum posts, discussions, etc., written by people about the website.** For businesses, there are many sources of reputation information and reviews. Here are some examples: Yelp, Better Business Bureau (or BBB, a non-profit organization that focuses on the trustworthiness of businesses and charities), Amazon,

and Google Product Search. You can try searching on specific sites to find reviews. For example, you can try [ibm site:bbb.org] or ["ibm.com" site:bbb.org].

Note: You will sometimes find high ratings on the Better Business Bureau website because there is very little data on the business, not because the business has a positive reputation. However, low ratings on BBB are usually the result of multiple unresolved complaints. Consider very low ratings on the BBB site to be evidence of a negative reputation.

4. **See if there is a Wikipedia article or news article from a well-known news site.** News articles and Wikipedia articles can help you learn about a company and may include information specific to reputation, such as awards and other forms of recognition.

"This is pretty complicated," I said, looking up from my laptop.

"It seems that way at first," Dave explained. "But again, those search queries are all really logical in their structure. Once you know how to write them, it's quite a simple process."

Just then, I received an instant message from Helen on WhatsApp: *How's it going?*

Dave dipped back into his own emails for a second, giving me time to reply: *Good, I think. Looks like I'm starting to understand this stuff. Cocktails tonight?* Helen asked.

Not a chance! Isn't two nights in a row a bit much, even for you!?! Not when I got a raise and a promotion today!!!! she replied.

We'll see. Now leave me alone. I'm in a meeting. I hit Send before realizing I'd neglected to acknowledge her news. I typed quickly: *Oh, and congratulations. I'm really happy for you.* I turned my attention back to Dave, who looked up from his laptop. "I didn't realize that you could look up what Google had to say about companies," I said. "I guess I need to start by taking a look at what people are saying about DesignSpace online. I did a bit of research when I was looking for the job, but because I couldn't find much online, I kind of stopped."

David looked at me with a slight grin.

"Sure, but if you couldn't find the right information from Google, there's virtually no chance that an end user is going to be able to locate DesignSpace online without a great deal of digging and searching. That explains why the company shows up third on the results, even though we were searching by its exact brand name."

Wow. I'd been ready to accept a challenge when I took on this job, but a Herculean struggle? That was something else altogether—and maybe more than I bargained for.

"The next important thing I'd like you to consider is the website's helpfulness," Dave said. "Google wants to provide the most helpful answer to any online search. So, once you've done the hard work and tried to figure out what your customer's intent would be when visiting the DesignSpace website, you have to design the site—and all the pages that comprise it—to be as helpful as possible in answering those questions.

"This all goes back to striking the right alignment with the website's purpose," he continued. "Is the purpose to sell something? Is it to inform, entertain, or educate someone? Maybe it's a combination of two or more of those intentions. In DesignSpace's case, we have a bunch of different websites at play, in addition to the one promoting Joe's core commercial office furniture business. Although we've only been focusing on the one so far, a couple of these different concepts can come in to play to help make us successful."

I nodded, wondering why it had taken Dave so long to bring that up. During one of my interviews, Joe had mentioned that, back a few years ago when domain squatting was all the rage, he'd bought a ton of different domains and set up single-page websites on each one. "Do you know anything about that?"

Dave laughed. "Yeah, Joe's not the only domain squatter out there. At one point, I had several thousand websites, all in the same niche. Some went on to be quite good performers, but the rest were just a waste of time and money."

"That's not exactly what you're supposed to do, is it?" I asked, offering a smile of my own.

"No," said Dave, shaking his head, "but the most exciting thing about doing business online is that the rules keep changing. The best long-term strategy, however, is to provide the most value to your particular industry or audience niche, and to allow users to give feedback on their experience. Google will then take that information and reward the websites that are genuinely trying to help their end users."

Dave closed the screen on his laptop, stood up, and started pacing again.

"Let's go back to the beginning," he said. "What is the purpose of the website? Let's use DesignSpace's business-to-business website as an example. On the site, the purpose is to obtain sales leads. Have a look at the current homepage and tell me if you think it's helpful or not."

I pulled up the website and quickly scanned it from top to bottom.

Dave came around from the other side of the table and peered over my shoulder.

"I noticed that you scrolled up and down the page, scanning. What were your first impressions?"

I looked at the page carefully. "Well, the layout is pretty bad. There are images, and some text that could be helpful, but from a quick scan I'm not sure exactly what I'm supposed to do. There's not much of a call to action, and the navigability is pretty lame."

Dave nodded. "And?"

"Well," I continued, "I'm not sure about the site's purpose, how it's supposed to perform, or how I'm supposed to go about getting any additional information. I guess I'm supposed to click on the navigation bar at the top and maybe go to the Contact Us page to try to find information about the products and services, but that doesn't seem very efficient. It certainly doesn't seem like something an end user would do."

Dave walked back around to the other side of the table.

"So, from an end-user perspective, you weren't able to find the information you were looking for, at least not at a first glance. That means you'd either go to the Contact Us page or, more likely, bounce back to Google and not come back to the site. Is that fair to say?"

I stuck to a nod, because what I really wanted to say was that their old marketing guy, John, should have been fired a *long* time ago.

"How many people do you think experience the same thing? They come to the website—when they can actually find it—and get frustrated because they can't locate the information they want, so they bounce off?"

"Probably quite a few," I said.

Dave flipped open his laptop again, even more animated now than usual.

"Joe had the foresight to set up Google Analytics on his homepage, and I've been taking a look at some of his traffic numbers. The figures are pretty low, but the site's been around for a while, so it's got a bit of authority. But the scary thing is the amount of people who come to a page and bounce right back off. In Google Analytics, this is recorded as a *bounce rate*, which gives you a percentage of total visitors who looked at your site and then left. Joe's bounce rate for the B2B site is in the 90 percent range, which is terrible given that he has only a small amount of traffic to begin with. Of that little bit of traffic, only one out of ten people actually sticks around and explores more than one page on the site."

So, not only can nobody find this website, they straight up hate it when they get there. I wondered if Dave had any other good news for me today.

"Google favors sites that have more information and more pages because they're deemed to be more helpful," he added. "So, a good rule of thumb is the more pages the better. But the pages can't just be filler, or images, or dead ends. They have to provide relevant, useful information associated with the topic and purpose of the website. Beginning with DesignSpace's B2B website, there's a number of different things that we can do to help improve the page performance by increasing the helpfulness of the site. And yep, you guessed it. I have notes on this too."

Dave flipped his bullet points to me in an email.

Cheat Sheet – Examples of Helpful Page Purposes:

- to share information about a topic
- to share personal or social information
- to share pictures, videos, or other forms of media
- to express an opinion or point of view
- to entertain
- to sell products or services
- to allow users to post questions for other users to answer
- to allow users to share files or download software

"I'm getting hungry, how about you?" he asked.

"I could definitely eat," I replied, checking the time on my phone. It was already 12:30. I guess time flies when you have a very limited grasp of your new job!

"Great, do you like Mexican? A new fast-food place just opened around the corner."

"Sounds good to me."

We headed out to navigate Manhattan's busy midtown streets. I was going to have lunch with my new, kind-of-boss. I wondered what Dave would be like "off the clock." More important, I wondered if he'd pick up the tab!

Chapter 4 Takeaways

✓ Key questions to determine web page searchability and potential ranking: Is this page relevant? Is this page helpful? Is this page trustworthy?

✓ Your homepage should be the most relevant result that matches the specific user intent of people searching for your company. The goal: to produce a relevant, topical, helpful, and high-quality result

✓ Google wil avoid any attempts to manipulate search engine results, and will blacklist any individual or organization attempting to artificially boost their rankings

✓ Search engine rankings are largely determined by the quality and quantity of relevant content on your website

✓ Posting thought leadership or newsworthy blog content is an important aspect of search ranking success for an organization, helping Google determine that your organization is a formidable authority on a particular subject

✓ Blogs and website copy should be written to engage and inform your target audience—not satisfy the Google bots

✓ Website trust is determined both by the Google bots, as well as individual users who visit a website, read it, and comment about it on other sites

✓ Other points that influence search rankings: 3rd party references, reviews

✓ Website design should be reflective of users' intent. Do they want to know, go or buy?

✓ Google favors sites that have more information and more pages because they're deemed to be more helpful. But pages must be relevant, containing useful information associated with the topic and purpose of the website

Chapter 5

Dave sat down at the table with his tray. His plate was covered by a massive enchilada, sitting alongside a large glass of water.

I sat across from him, ready to dive into a delicious-looking order of fish tacos. But before I took my first bite, I thanked him for paying for my lunch (*mystery solved!*).

"No problem," he said. "It's the least I can do for making you listen to me talk about website design and SEO."

We exchanged smiles and I dug in.

"So, tell me," Dave started, "how'd you find out about the job at DesignSpace?"

"I saw the job posting on LinkedIn," I replied. "I'd been trying to get back into marketing after my internships didn't lead me to any decent full-time jobs. I'd been working as a barista in the meantime, and looked like a good opportunity. I also really like art and design, so I thought a company that builds office furniture and designs spaces might be a good fit."

"That's interesting. Did you study design at university, or ever work in the field?"

"No, my mom is an interior decorator, so I guess you could say I kind of grew up close to the industry. DesignSpace offered a little bit of everything, and Joe was offering pretty decent money and the culture seemed solid, so I thought I'd take a chance. Can I be honest about something?"

"Sure," Dave said, resting his fork on his plate and leaning in.

"I'm feeling a bit overwhelmed at the moment. In fact, I think I might be in a little over my head."

"I completely understand," he answered reassuringly. "I'm sorry for blitzing you with so many new concepts and terms. I probably should have taken things a bit slower, but as you learned in the meeting with Raj, this company is in desperate need of marketing help. I didn't think we could offer to hold off any longer, so I decided to throw you into the deep end and see how you swam. If it helps, I think you're doing great so far."

"Thanks. DesignSpace isn't going to go bankrupt, is it?"

"No, you're going to get paid, don't worry." He smiled. "There's no need to worry about bankruptcy, but the company is not growing nearly as fast as it could—if at all. The challenge for companies like DesignSpace is that when they ignore marketing for so long, or do it poorly, they have to spend a lot of time and money to catch up with their competitors. It winds up being far more expensive than simply making investments on an ongoing basis."

"I was poking around and noticed that companies like Office Solutions have great websites with tons of content, great social media accounts, you name it."

"Yep, that's exactly what I mean," Dave said, taking another bite of his lunch. "Once you start to fall behind your closest competitors—in this case, companies like Office Solutions and Patel Workplace Designers—it's very hard to catch up, although thankfully not impossible. Like I said, a lot of companies don't realize that you have to invest in this stuff on an ongoing basis, not once every few years. I can explain more about budgeting in the next couple of days if you like, but I usually push my clients to spend at least 5 percent, and sometimes as much as 10 percent, of their annual revenue on marketing. But maybe I'm just biased . . ."

"No," I interjected. "That makes a lot of sense. I think DesignSpace could have been a $20 million company by now if they'd had the right marketing help. The furniture looks great, and I understand our designers are really talented, though I haven't met any of them yet."

"We'll have to get Joe to make some introductions when we get back to the office. You know, it sounds like you're thinking like a CEO. I like your ideas about doubling the company's revenue. Joe would, too!"

We both finished our meals and made small talk about the latest movies and our favorite TV shows before starting our walk back to the office.

"How did you became a consultant," I asked, figuring I might as well learn a bit more about the guy I would be working with for the foreseeable future.

"I got frustrated," he answered.

"Um, with what, exactly?"

"I worked for a couple of companies in succession that kept making foolish digital marketing mistakes—mistakes that were costing them key opportunities to grow and succeed. The owners thought they knew marketing and wouldn't take any advice. In some cases, those missed opportunities resulted in them falling on hard financial times."

"So you decided to do something about it?"

"I guess you could say that," Dave replied. "I thought I could put my expertise and experience to better use running my own company, so I did, and haven't looked back since." We arrived at the building just as Raj was leaving. He held the door for us both.

"Still coming to softball this week?" he asked Dave.

"Should be," Dave answered. They traded a few other comments before parting ways. I still found their relationship puzzling: ready to kill each other during a finance meeting, but friends outside of the office.

After a short elevator ride we made it to the floor that housed DesignSpace and about a dozen other companies. It was a millennial's dream work environment—an open-concept work environment, a games room, a full kitchen and fun meeting spaces that actually made you want to go to work.

We walked through the office and back to the boardroom, where Dave quickly resumed our earlier conversation about website helpfulness.

"I sent you examples of the many ways that web pages can be helpful, so let's expand on that discussion," he began.

I flipped open my laptop and scanned the bullet points in his earlier email.

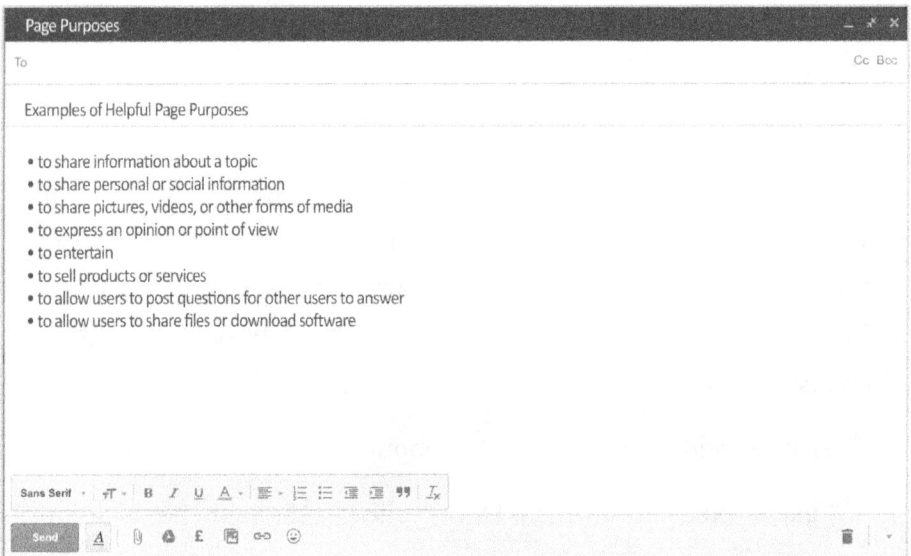

Page Purposes   _ ⟋ ✕

To   Cc Bcc

Examples of Helpful Page Purposes

- to share information about a topic
- to share personal or social information
- to share pictures, videos, or other forms of media
- to express an opinion or point of view
- to entertain
- to sell products or services
- to allow users to post questions for other users to answer
- to allow users to share files or download software

Sans Serif ᐧ ₸ ᐧ B I U A ᐧ ☰ ᐧ ⠿ ⠿ ⠿ ⠿ 〝 Iₓ

Send   A   ▯ ⬤ £ ▣ ∞ ☺   🗑 ᐧ ▾

"None of those purposes have to be used in isolation," he explained. "You can provide information about a topic *and* allow users to post questions for other users to answer. A good example of this can be found at Moz.com, which has information about SEO, as well as large discussion forums with related questions. Part of their business model is helping others to get better at online marketing, so hosting a forum for that particular audience makes perfect sense."

I quickly keyed *Moz.com* into my browser and scanned the company's homepage.

"Some companies also like to try to bridge content gaps by including plug-ins for Twitter and Facebook on their websites, with the idea of syndicating content from social networks and appearing to be up-to-date," Dave continued. "This is an okay solution, but it doesn't actually provide much in the way of attribution for the content. To put that in English, as far as anyone's concerned, including Google, the content isn't recognized as having originated from your website—and that's never a good thing."

Dave carried on, reiterating why it's so important for companies—both business to business (B2B) and business to consumer (B2C)—to establish authority in their respective areas of business using strong content in addition to the best practices he was outlining. Attributing content that's published on other websites or channels back to an originating website is a best practice that should be followed whenever possible.

"I look at it this way," he said. "If you find it helpful to use an automated feed, go for it. But you have to bear in mind that as soon as anyone posts anything associated with your company, like a review, that feed information will show on your website. And as with any automation tool, leaving it alone and unchecked is a dangerous idea."

"So you need to moderate anything that shows up on your website."

"Precisely," Dave said. "It can be a bit time-consuming, for sure, but it's worth the effort. I've seen companies end up with some really vicious and inappropriate remarks in the comment sections on their blog pages, for example, and you wouldn't believe the kind of advertising and other garbage that can show up when you're least expecting it."

"I can't believe what trolls will write to disrupt websites and just be annoying," I interjected.

"More than just annoying," Dave pointed out. "That kind of nonsense can really compromise a company's brand, and in a worst-case scenario, lead to legal challenges or digital security breaches. That doesn't happen often, but when it does, it can bring a company to its knees."

I took a second to jot down some notes. *The real challenge, as I was coming to see it, was to create pages on DesignSpace's website that would establish authority in our core topic areas—obvious things like office design, space efficiency, and employee collaboration—while also conveying a sense of trust to our target clientele.*

"This all ties into your content marketing strategy," added Dave. "Companies write e-books, post a lot of content on their blogs, attempt to interview notable people or invite them to write guest posts—sometimes that's other consultants like me, or even customers that businesses want to feature in some way, like maybe in a case study—and they try to have this content published on other industry-related blogs or websites. The general idea is to broadcast out as much information to the world as possible. There are many different tactics you can use to achieve this outcome."

"Sounds like a lot of work," I said, wondering how many late nights I'd have to log writing blogs and tweeting. I stifled the urge to grumble; *after all, I'd been looking for a challenge . . .*

"It is, and the strategy can work if it's deployed properly," Dave explained. "But you have to bear in mind that people can get tired of being bombarded by information from your company. You have to engage in a conversation with your end users in order to be helpful and responsive to them. Done right, this approach allows you to gain important insights into how you should be developing your marketing program, not to mention improving your products and services."

"You're saying the content can actually be a tool we can use to learn more about our customers and their needs?"

"Exactly," Dave replied. "The real trick is to make sure the content follows some key rules: it should be tied to a current trend or news related to your industry; it should mean something to your audience; it has to interest them in some way; and it has to enlighten them. It's on that last point that a lot of companies fall flat."

"How so?"

"They think that just because they've written a blog or a white paper or something of interest to them that it's also going to appeal to their target audience—and that's not always the case. The social media era has turned us all into publishers, if we choose to take on that role. But we also have to think like smart publishers, or like journalists, and make sure that the content we're producing makes sense. And it should always help our companies build stronger brands, deepen client relationships, and sell more. That's how this is all supposed to function, at least in theory."

"Makes sense, but does it actually work?" I wondered out loud.

"Good question. The short answer is yes. As we know, the vast majority of customer research on any particular company is done online before that customer ever reaches out to the company. I would estimate that number at around 60 percent. So, the idea is that the more information you have out in the cloud and on the Internet, the better, because prospective customers will be more likely to stumble across your information. This has worked exceptionally well for companies like HubSpot. com, which are pioneers in inbound marketing. Nowadays, it's all about earning the trust of your target clientele or audience, and relevant content is one way to do that."

My eyes darted back to my laptop, where I quickly started browsing HubSpot's homepage. I'd heard of the company and knew they were popular, but I hadn't really given their products and services much thought until now. "I guess this is a great strategy if it aligns with your company's goals, as well as the information or outcome your end users need," I offered.

"Good insight," Dave stood up, apparently to stretch his legs. "You're right again, and this approach does work out for most companies that try it. But the big question is how to develop a similar yet customized strategy to help DesignSpace achieve its digital marketing results."

I stopped taking notes for second and thought about it.

"I guess there are some similarities between what HubSpot is trying to do and what we're trying to do here," I suggested. "We're both business-to-business focused companies, and we're both trying to get people to take a particular action when they discover us online. But I think the similarities pretty much end there. What Joe is trying to accomplish is very different from what HubSpot is trying to accomplish, so I would think that a helpful page for us would probably look quite different from anything you'd see on HubSpot.com."

Dave nodded. "You're very much on the right track, but remember, there are some common elements for all landing pages that can make them helpful, useful, and authoritative."

My inbox pinged and in came another email of bullet points from Dave.

Cheat Sheet – Ten Essential Landing Page Elements for High Conversion Rates

- Logo
- Headline
- Offer
- Descriptive Copy
- Product Presentation
- Calls to Action
- Trust/Confidence Building
- Contact Information
- Links to More Information (Secondary Site Content)
- Template Elements (Main Site Content)

Not only are these elements important on their own, they have to work with each other. Take into account the following:

- Relevance
- Quality
- Location
- Proximity
- Prominence

"There's a lot in there, so let's start at the beginning," Dave said, probably noticing a familiar, overwhelmed look creeping across my face. This whole process was beginning to feel like an extremely fast-tracked university course, but without the right amount of study time, and with a company's future basically hanging in the balance. "So, what is a landing page?" Dave asked rhetorically, before answering his own question.

"A landing page is a page on your website that matches up and answers a particular user query in an authoritative, trustworthy, and helpful way. Most of the time, a landing page is designed to serve a certain purpose. This purpose is often to drive sales through online conversions, but it can also be to inform or interact with end users—like what we were just discussing with content marketing. Put another way, a landing page is the place where traffic lands on your website after a potential client or audience member arrives from some other site. In most cases, this traffic will come from Google or another search engine."

"Got it," I said, furiously typing notes on my laptop.

"No need to jot this stuff down, I'll have an expanded version of the cheat sheet that I'll email to you later, with much more information," Dave stated, much to my relief. Ever since university, I've always found it more beneficial to simply sit back and listen to a speaker rather than trying to take extensive notes. But maybe that's just me!

"What's another reason why a landing page important?" Dave continued. "A well-designed landing page is especially important for paid search. If you're paying to attract targeted visitors to your site, you should design every page with an end goal in mind. That end goal can be a user performing some desired action, or turning your site into a resource for information. Maybe it's something else entirely, but whatever your goal, the page should be designed to achieve that desired outcome."

He reiterated that a page's ranking comes back to its helpfulness and utility to its target audience. "If the content is useful, Google will view it as being more valuable," he pointed out. "If you're designing a landing page to use with paid search, for example, the utility of the page is important because the user will need to perform whatever specific action is required to support the company's specific marketing effort. Utility is the most important aspect of search engine quality for paid and organic search, and is therefore the most important thing for you to think about when designing landing pages.

"The other major factor to consider when designing a landing page is user intent," he continued. "You need to take into account the search terms, and the likely user intent of that search, so that your landing page becomes as useful as possible to that end user. That's why it's a good idea to design for one or both of what we call 'action intent' and 'information intent'.

With action intent, users will want to accomplish a goal or engage in an activity, such as downloading software, playing an online game, sending flowers, or maybe finding entertaining video clips. You get the idea. These are what we call do queries, indicating that users want to engage in a specific action."

I listened with a growing sense of confidence. What Dave was saying was really pretty logical, but it was clearly important to know how the various components work together in order to make sure your website is found by a target audience or clientele.

"Information intent is a little bit different," Dave carried on. "In this case, users will want to find insights or details specific to their end goal. These are *'I want to know'* queries, where users will attempt to educate themselves in some way by locating information. Helpful pages have high-quality, authoritative, and comprehensive information about the user's desired query."

"So, the bottom line is that a landing page is a page on your website that matches and answers a particular user query in an authoritative, trustworthy, and helpful way," I summarized. I typed as I spoke; cheat sheets were great, but I wanted to get this down in my own words.

"You should be the one explaining this stuff, not me—you're really getting it now," Dave said with a wide grin. "Now that you have an idea why people are coming to your page—it matches up as a solution to their query—let's look at the elements one by one . . . "

Dave paused when his phone buzzed. "I have a call from another client," he said. "I'm going to flip this list over to you and let you give it a read. I'll be back in fifteen minutes."

Dave answered the phone and simultaneously emailed over another batch of notes. *I could write a book with all of the stuff he's providing,* I thought, but I wasn't about to give him a hard time over it. I wasn't quite sure where I'd be at this point without his thoroughness.

Logo

Your logo serves several functions on a landing page. First, it's there to establish trust. Any brand that is worthwhile has a well-designed logo displayed prominently. This logo also serves another purpose as part of your main website content: in order to establish your overall website as a reliable source of information, and as trustworthy, you need to have the ability to go to the homepage of your website simply by clicking on the logo, or including a Home button as a key part of the page.

Headline

The headline of your landing page is important both from an end-user experience point of view, and from a search engine experience perspective. If you're using paid search to drive traffic to a particular landing page, for example, the headline will be used to determine the relevance of the landing page and should therefore align with both your ad and the keyword that you've used to drive traffic to the landing page in the first place. This will improve your quality score and search engine results in an advertising auction.

The headline is also very important from a user perspective because people need to know where they've landed and if it's relevant to their initial search query. Clearly defining what the page is about at the top will help keep visitors on the site and reduce your bounce rates.

Offer

The offer on your landing page is very important, especially if you're trying to spark a particular action on the part of visitors to the website. Creating a sense of urgency, giving special discounts, or simply describing what people will receive if they purchase your product or service are all common ways to state an offer.

Descriptive Copy

Descriptive copy on the landing page is important for a variety of reasons. Keep in mind that the end goal for Google is to provide results that are helpful and useful, while also matching a user's search query. Having text on the page that the Google bot can read is important to ensure that you're delivering an adequate landing page experience for your end users.

Text on the page that describes what it's about also helps people navigate the page more effectively—and get the information they're seeking. This helps to exponentially improve the user experience, keep users engaged, and hopefully encourage them to spend more time on your website. Longer time-on-site is another positive indicator that Google takes into account when determining a website's trust rating.

Product Presentation

The main goal with product presentation is to help visitors determine what your web page is about. If you're selling a particular product or service, you should have a prominent and attractive product picture. Images are high-converting assets on any landing page. You also have to make sure that you're utilizing proper alt text (included when an element can't be rendered on a web page) and labeling, and are captioning your images so Google can recognize what the photo is about. If you aren't trying to sell a particular product or service, you should still include images for a better user experience, which can be part of the product presentation.

Calls to Action

Your landing page is designed to prompt users to perform a particular action. The more obvious and clear you can make this desired action, the better. Multiple calls to action (like a 'more information' button) are very important if the user is required to scroll down to see more of your descriptive text and product images. A good rule of thumb is to have one call to action for each screen when scrolling down.

A second thing to bear in mind when you're talking about calls to action is the need to present attractive text while also utilizing specific information associated with your messaging. Some call-to-action buttons have been so overused that people simply ignore them. We recommend action-based words in your call-to-action buttons, such as "Get Started." It's important to experiment with terms because any call to action will only maintain its effectiveness for so long before visitors begin to ignore it as well.

Trust/Confidence Building

Trust and confidence building elements are the most important items on your landing page. This secondary content is important both from a machine perspective as well as from an end-user perspective.

From a machine perspective, Google will trust third-party reviews before it trusts the information on your website or landing page. If you can link to third-party citations and references, this makes a page stronger from a Google perspective. From an end-user experience perspective, having recognized company logos and testimonials with information provided about happy customer experiences go a long way when trying to sell a product. The vast majority of product research for online purchases is now done on third-party websites and social networks. The more frequently you can reference strong referrals recommending your product or service, the better.

Contact Information

Contact information is very important from both a landing page perspective and as part of the core content on your website. This is also an element you should use to help gain the trust of the visitor and the machine, underlining the purpose of your website and the legitimacy of your company. Contact information such as hours of operation, store or office locations, and multiple contact numbers or email addresses are key to establishing good rapport and earning a good reputation online.

Links to More Information (Secondary Site content)

Circling back around to the original design and purpose of your page from a Google perspective, having helpful links that push visitors toward more and relevant information is key to improving Google rankings, as well as to establishing whether or not your pages are helpful, useful, and authoritative.

Some companies or individuals recommend omitting anything from your landing page other than the desired call to action. They argue that such an approach helps to avoid distraction on the part of visitors. This raises a number of red flags, the first of which is that the original website isn't strong enough to convert visitors, but also that their objective is to manipulate the end user into performing a particular action. There's nothing more annoying than getting to a page that might be of interest only to find that you are unable to learn anything else about the company from that page. The only option at that point is to use your web browser's "back button" to continue navigating the site, or to bounce back to Google. The back button is the enemy of all online marketers, especially if you've paid for someone to come to your landing page.

Template Elements (Main Site Content)

Examples of some important template elements include the top navigation bar, as well as the footer on your website. These elements link to more information internally, as well as to other information such as your privacy policy, product return terms, or customer service information, all of which are important indicators that allow Google to establish just how trustworthy and relevant your website is from an end-user perspective.

These template elements are especially important if your site involves an e-commerce store, or some other function that requires users to engage in a financial transaction. In these cases, having searchable contact information and other key elements is very important.

With this basic understanding of the necessary elements, let's take a look at how they work together.

Relevance

Relevance is very important both from an organic and paid search perspective. The user's query, as keyed into Google's search box, should closely align with the information and relevance of the landing page, especially if you're paying for clicks to drive users to that page.

For paid search, Google takes into account your keywords, your ad text, and your landing page experience to come up with an overall quality score associated with a particular keyword. The higher the quality score, the more relevant the landing page experience and the less money you need to pay to have visitors come to that landing page. But perhaps most important, the information on the page should be relevant to its various components. This simply means that any product images should be accurately reflected in the descriptive copy, and the product or service being sold should align with the site's purpose. This relevance will improve the overall user experience and, as a result, prompt Google to place your website higher in search rankings.

Quality

This is a much more subjective measure of website relevance, but some simple rules of thumb will help you improve the quality of the landing page experience. Bearing in mind that the purpose of the page should be to provide a helpful, useful, and authoritative experience, simple misspellings of words, poor-quality copy, blurry or small pictures, and a lack of secondary content to support these pages will result in a poor user-quality score. From a machine perspective, featuring images on your website is acceptable, but they must be labeled properly. Otherwise, your page may get a lower quality estimate due to the fact that the search engine can't "read" the photos you've posted.

Location

The location of all of these elements is just as important as having them on the page in the first place. Some companies try to go for a unique layout, but that often serves to confuse users who were expecting to find items such as a Home button, or the logo in the top corner of the website. Placing the latter in the bottom corner, for example, may seem like a cute design idea, but is never a smart decision.

The second point worth noting is that not everyone will scroll down through a web page. A well-designed page should have all of the necessary elements "above the fold"—or within the first screen shot when they arrive on your landing page, if possible.

This optimized user experience is very important on devices such as laptops, smartphones, and tablets. A responsive website that identifies what browser and the type of devices audience members are using to visit your site is crucial. This helps improve the end-user experience immensely, and will enable you to have your landing page elements presented to them clearly and effectively upon arrival.

Proximity

The proximity of any of these elements is also important. Certain elements—such as trust-building elements, for example—should be grouped together, with clear divisions and indicators if there is more information to scroll to. Proximity also plays an important role in overall attractiveness and design utility. If a page is composed solely of text and is not broken up by calls to action or product pictures, this can create user challenges. Even most encyclopedia-based websites, like Wikipedia, break up their content with photos and citations. From a utility perspective, if there's a particular action that you want a user to take, the action should be in close proximity to the information they require to make that decision.

Prominence

The final element is prominence. This is especially important when taking into account the various design elements and core content of your website. It's up to you to determine how prominently you want to feature links to your privacy information, as well as other content in template elements, versus how large you want your product photo to be. In any case, it's very important that you have a prominent call to action if you require a particular action on that page. We recommend a contrast color that stands out from the rest of the information on the page and a clear label to help customers engage in a specific action.

✓ Rule of thumb: to maintain a coherent marketing program, expect to make consistent investments of 5 to 10 per cent of your organization's annual revenue

✓ Automated content feeds can be convenient, but also risky—when not curated, feeds can sometimes display unsavoury or off-brand content

✓ Important rules for producing strong content: it should be tied to a current trend or news related to your industry; it should mean something to your audience; it has to interest your audience in some way; it should engage them

✓ A landing page is a page on your website that answers a particular user query in an authoritative, trustworthy, and helpful way

✓ Utility is the most important aspect of search engine quality for paid and organic search, and is therefore the most important consideration when designing landing pages

✓ Two types of user intent: action and information

✓ With action intent, users will want to accomplish a goal or engage in an activity

✓ With information intent, users will want to find insights or details specific to their end goal

Chapter 6

"Sorry about that," Dave said as he walked back into the boardroom. "We had a small client emergency last week and we're still feeling the aftershocks. So, where were we?"

"I just made it through those notes on important landing page elements," I said. "There was a lot of information in there."

"Yeah, there's a lot to learn," Dave replied, leaning back in his chair. He removed his glasses and rubbed his eyes. "Okay, let's take a break from the laptops for a second." Just then, Joe burst into the boardroom. "Can I see you both in my office for a second," he asked, his voice brimming with excitement.

"Sure thing," Dave said, looking over at me and offering a slight shrug.

We walked down to Joe's office and, once inside, he closed the door behind us.

"Great news," he started. "Tina in sales has made major headway in her discussions with Siemens. I'm sure you guys are familiar with them." He smiled.

"They're a grocery chain, right?" Dave replied.

"You're too quick for me," Joe snapped back with a chuckle. "Well, Siemens – the global company - is very close to signing a two-year contract with DesignSpace, to the tune of about $5 million. This would be huge for us. But Tina says it would be beneficial to have a refreshed website that better displays our furniture products and showcases our design capabilities. We really need to tell a coherent brand story and showcase the strength of our team."

I was keying notes into my laptop, heart racing at the thought of the company landing such a major new client.

Dave leaned forward. "So, what you're saying is—"

"What I'm saying," Joe interjected, "is that we need this new website live ASAP. Think we can make it happen?"

"It all depends on your definition of ASAP," said Dave.

"Thirty days?"

I swallowed hard and looked down at my keyboard. My fingers stopped moving as I tried to figure out how to respond. I wanted to sound eager and showcase my can-do attitude, but a month didn't seem like much time at all given my inexperience. And I still wasn't sure how long Dave was going to be hanging around, or whether he'd been hired to do the heavy lifting on the website, or just to consult.

"Um, I guess so," I answered sheepishly.

"A month might be pushing it, but I know a web development firm that can probably help out on the project," Dave offered. "I can make a few calls and we can get the ball rolling sooner rather than later."

"Perfect," Joe replied. "The other point Tina stressed was the need to make the website mobile friendly. It's a bit of an optics thing, seeing as the Siemens folks are constantly using smartphones and tablets during meetings, at their desks—pretty much everywhere."

Joe, still standing, turned toward me. "Sorry to put the pressure on you like this, but we need this account."

"Well, that's why I'm here," I answered, *hoping the ground would open and swallow me whole.*

"Awesome." A split second after gaining our buy-in for this Herculean task, Joe moved on to asking questions about how everything was going on the marketing front. After Dave provided a bit of detail about the topics we'd been discussing, Joe asked me to remind him about completing introductions to the rest of the team. We exchanged a few pleasantries, and then Dave and I marched back to the boardroom.

It felt like I was taking a long walk off a very short pier.

"So," Dave began, easing into his boardroom chair, "what do you think?"

"I'm not sure what to think," I replied.

"Welcome to the fast-paced world of marketing. Where anything's possible—and chances are, your boss will ask you to do it in less than half the time that should reasonably be allotted to complete said task."

He was smiling when he said that. I wasn't.

"I noticed that you're using the latest android-based device," he said. "How do you like it?"

I looked over at my phone, sitting next to my laptop on the table, wrapped in a creative case that I'd designed myself. "I love it," I said. "I basically live on this thing—when it's not in the shop for repairs after another accidental drop on my part. A new one is coming out in a few weeks, though, so I'm not sure if I'm going to stick with this or upgrade."

"You might want to opt for an unbreakable model, or at least buy accident insurance," Dave said, smiling. "Yeah, maybe I'll do that," I replied tersely. I wasn't in the mood for Dave's humor at this point.

"Do you think you'll look for a model with the same size screen, or maybe something slightly different?"

I thought about it for a second. "I'm not sure. I think the new model is about the same size, but it's quite a bit faster, and has more memory."

Dave nodded. "Let's take a bit of a break from Google on your desktop and talk a little bit about search results on your phone. Nowadays we live online, and we're basically tethered to our phones 24/7, just like you mentioned a few minutes ago. You fit a pretty typical usage profile for your age demographic. I'm older than you, but even I use my smartphone as an alarm clock, stopwatch, health barometer—and basically for everything else in my life I need to keep track of or organize." I could totally relate. *I really don't know what I'd do without my phone. It's my work tool, my entertainment, and sometimes even my salvation—like when I text Helen and get her to rescue me from a bad dinner date by pretending to be an emotional wreck after a pretend breakup with a fictional boyfriend.*

"Not long ago, end users and consumers had to consciously get their computer booted up, log in, and then search for specific terms," Dave explained.

"I don't mean to totally date myself, but we've come a long way since the days of dial-up Internet," he said, chuckling to himself.

"I remember dial-up. My parents switched to high-speed when I was ten or so."

"Okay, now you're making me feel old," Dave shot back. I could only smile.

"Back in October 2015, Google announced that there were more searches conducted on mobile devices than there were on desktops. I can't really quantify just how great an impact that change has had on the marketing industry. This trend has transformed how marketing departments are structured, which leaders are chosen for which roles, and the expertise levels of the employees they hire. It all comes back to the idea that mobile is the future, though desktops still play a huge role for now. I personally believe they'll continue to be relevant for a while, simply because their screen size provides certain user experiences that aren't yet possible on mobile devices."

"I have a friend who's a user-experience designer," I explained. "She makes a fortune and all she does is work on mobile apps."

"That's not surprising," Dave said. "UX designers are in high demand right now because companies like DesignSpace are determined to enhance, or even try to perfect, the experience their clientele or audience enjoys when visiting any of their digital platforms. And they want that audience to have unique experiences on each one. This represents a whole new way of looking at mobile."

Dave went on to explain how huge ad campaigns for events like the Super Bowl used to impact a brand's sales and influence customer behavior. Now, the story's quite different. Organizations used to focus on creating huge moments when their brands could shine on a world stage. But that was when the journey to a customer purchase was mostly linear, marketing was time-consuming, and the information you could glean about a customer segment was limited (which stifled a company's ability to micro-target). Those big ad campaigns still have an impact, he added, but thanks to content marketing, social media campaigns, experiential initiatives, and a whole host of other tactics that marketing departments can leverage year-round to deliver results, the impact of any single (and expensive) campaign is lessened.

"We have to recognize how our ability to 'live' online has changed the way we interact with companies," he carried on. "Let's focus on DesignSpace as an example. Whenever a need arises or a thought crosses a customer's mind to research a potential engagement with the company, or to compare it to other furniture and design firms, that customer needs to be able to act on that need immediately, wherever they happen to be. It's a little less imperative on the B2B front, of course, because companies tend to take more time when making purchasing decisions. But for B2C organizations, a lousy mobile presence can destroy sales."

Dave paused for a minute to let that sink in, then continued. "That idea even extends to companies that have physical stores. Google recently published research indicating that 82 percent of people with smartphones use them while actually in a store to compare prices—and that number is growing."

I do that all the time, I thought. *And I usually find cheaper prices on websites like Amazon,* but sometimes I'll buy in-store anyways because I'm a sucker for impulse buys. Most of the time, though, I'll hold off and purchase whatever it is later to save a few dollars.

"We have to realize that consumers are using information from all kinds of different channels to learn, discover, research, and ultimately buy products," Dave continued. "So it's no longer necessarily about where or how your business operates—be that online or in a bricks-and-mortar shop—but a combination of one brand and one brand message across many channels. That's especially important for a company like DesignSpace, which has an office furniture showroom, and an online design component."

"Our online office-design tool is pretty rudimentary," I pointed out.

"And that's one of the things we'll need to improve when this site gets rebuilt," Dave said. "Another major consideration is that context is king. People need to be given the right information or the right offer at the right time in the right location. If you use geo-targeting to send a customer an email about a big sale when they're near your store, for example, there's a much better chance that lead will convert into a sale. Social media is another major influencer on purchasing-decision behaviors, particularly because so many people research reviews or 'likes' before deciding which products to buy. This is all very important stuff for a B2C company—not quite as much for a B2B firm like DesignSpace, but it's all worth noting."

"It's good background information," I agreed. "Like I said, if I'm in a store shopping for something that I know I can get somewhere else or online, I always check for the best deal on my phone, and more than once I've gone up to the cash register and shown the customer service representative a comparable deal, only to have them price-match or even beat a competitor's price."

Dave nodded his approval. "Many retailers are making headway with mobile, but it's hard because there is such a massive amount of marketing messaging out there, and, at the end of the day, everybody seems to be offering the same thing. It really comes down to the story that needs to be told. It's less and less about a traditional TV spot or some other large-scale ad campaign, and even less about the direct-mail piece, email blast, or anything that's traditionally been used in one-size-fits-all campaigns. What you need are relevant campaigns that spur customer action."

"Is that why so many companies are trying to create ad campaigns with more interesting angles?" I asked.

"Definitely," Dave replied. "Mobile has changed the consumer decision-making journey forever. The story you just shared about your purchase journey reminds me of a story a friend told me a while back. She was in a grocery store trying to understand why two brands of a particular facial treatment differed in price by 50 percent—not only that, but the more expensive option came in a smaller package. Her gut instinct told her to go with the larger product for less money, but she pulled out her smartphone and searched for product reviews as she was standing in the store. After looking through a bunch of different reviews, she realized she'd be completely wasting her money and potentially not having a great experience by purchasing the cheaper option, so she actually bought the smaller, more expensive option and was quite happy with the product."

I told Dave the story of my friend Sonya, who had just gotten married. She'd been traveling, and was killing time between flights at the airport when she started thinking about her home-buying options. She wanted to know whether she and her fiancée, Jay, could afford a house in a neighborhood she loved. She decided to search for a mortgage calculator. When she discovered how expensive it would be to buy a home in that neighborhood, Sonya felt a bit overwhelmed and put her phone away. But having that search history saved allowed her to break up the search journey into a bunch of different steps. She started to research some local mortgage providers. And once she did that, she discovered there was a lender who would not only approve them for the mortgage that they needed, but would also arrange specialized financing and a payment structure that made it much more affordable. She figured that quick search in the airport probably saved her $50,000, all thanks to handy mobile technology. "I like to think of a mobile device as a shopping assistant," Dave said. "It can help you pick a product right up to the last second before a transaction, even when you're in a checkout line. But it can also work against you." He laughed. "I was in line at Costco one day and noticed a pressure washer I'd wanted for a while. After doing a quick price comparison, I realized it was a good deal and ended up spending an extra $200 to buy it then and there. My wife was not pleased."

"You win some and you lose some," I chuckled.

"Let's get back to DesignSpace," Dave said, laughing and shaking his head. "All of this brings me to another concern—showrooming."

"Showrooming?" I asked, fairly certain that yet another puzzled expression was plastered on my face.

"It's basically a retailer's worst fear," he explained. "Showrooming is what happens when consumers come into a brick-and-mortar store, look at a product and pick one they want, and then go online and buy it elsewhere for less."

"So there's a name for what we've just been talking about!" Who knew?

"Yes, but savvy brands see it differently. If you properly maintain your online presence and make sure your site is mobile-optimized—namely, that your results show up first in search rankings—this can be a tremendous advantage. As far as DesignSpace is concerned, we have to look at it as an opportunity to assist customers and give them access to the information they need about this company's furniture products or design services even when in the showroom. That has to be offered in conjunction with very high-touch service where people are available to answer questions and provide advice as needed."

"Okay," I said, "but what about when they're not in the showroom?"

Dave explained how people will search for products or services on their mobile devices no matter where they are. Quite often, that happens when they're at a competitor's store, office, or showroom. This, then, becomes a critical opportunity to reach these potential clients and attract them *away* from whatever site or store they are looking at and *to* DesignSpace.

Having a first-rate mobile site has other benefits, too. Still using DesignSpace as an example, Dave explained that it can make our sales reps' lives easier, since clients will often walk into the showroom already having researched the products, knowing what they need, and having formed opinions of what they like and don't like. All the sales team needs to do is offer advice as needed, help complete the sale, and possibly offer additional services, such as interior design and consulting. Having that user- and mobile-friendly site as a first point of contact can help us maximize profits and ensure our clients are happy with what they bought.

"That value-added customer experience is extremely important in a crowded industry like office furniture, where there's huge competition and plenty of options for DesignSpace's clients," Dave added. "And remember: we're talking about clients who are spending a lot of money on any given purchase order. This approach is also important in trying to develop a lifetime customer relationship—you can set their expectations before they get into the store with your online presence, and then meet or exceed that expectation with your products and services."

I let that sink in for a moment, then asked a question. "But aren't the decisions made with the help of mobile devices usually for small, impulse purchases, or of the commoditized kind? Like maybe when you're deciding on what kind of TV or laptop you want to buy, for example, and you want to research customer reviews."

"Not necessarily," Dave said. "These days, people are making big decisions online—like that story you told me about your friend researching mortgage brokers. They're also booking vacations or buying cars. A friend of mine is the manager of a Toyota dealership, and he told me recently that more and more people are ordering their products online. A salesperson will then drive the car to the person's house so they can sign the paperwork. We're talking about delivering $50,000 to $75,000 vehicles to customers who have never even seen, touched, or driven the car before. That's a *huge* change in the customer experience."

"I'll say. A friend of mine sent me an online test-drive of a car he was looking at buying. I thought it was crazy, but I think he may have actually bought it without driving the car himself. Instead, he relied on the review and the reaction of the driver in the video. It's not something that I would do, but I guess he was comfortable with it."

Dave and I shared a laugh on that one. "I guess I'm dating myself again, but when I was growing up, there was absolutely no way you'd ever buy a car without test-driving it at least once, if not two or three times. I'm sure we'll be able to do virtual reality test-drives in the future, assuming we're even allowed to drive at all."

"How very Star Trek," I quipped.

Dave steered our discussion back to all things mobile. "Let's get down to some of the nitty-gritty and talk about how we can help Joe improve DesignSpace's mobile searches."

I leaned back into my laptop to take notes.

"We have to understand that shoppers are using their smartphones to help them decide what to buy," Dave started. "There are five ways that we can help them make these decisions."

I heard the familiar ping from my inbox as a new message arrived. "Let me guess," I said. "You just emailed me another cheat sheet."

Dave stood up and began his customary pacing. "I'll give you a few minutes to read it over," he said.

Cheat Sheet – Five Ways to Improve Mobile Search

1. Identify the DesignSpace customers' "I want to buy" moments. We will likely need to do some physical research here, questioning clients in surveys or in the showroom, or consider hiring representative focus groups to determine how they're researching and making purchase decisions for products like these.

2. We have to make sure we are online and discoverable when clients are considering purchase decisions. We will have to develop a comprehensive strategy that works across as many channels as possible—search engines, video platforms such as YouTube, social media platforms—all while bearing in mind that consumers may prefer to do their shopping on-site, or even online when engaging with one of DesignSpace's competitors.

3. Once we've determined what clients are looking for, when they are looking for it, and where they are looking, we have to deliver a thorough sample of relevant messaging. We have to look at how people are researching answers to their top questions and the search terms they are using, and then create ads and content that provide helpful answers to those searches so that we appear first in rankings—or at least higher than our competitors.

4. Once customers have found us and we've delivered relevant information, we have to make sure that it's easy for them to make a purchase. The steps from research to decision to purchase should be simple and seamless. We should provide multiple ways to purchase. Whether that's buying online from our site or from a YouTube video, or making sure we have inventory in the showroom that they can search, we have to make this process as easy as possible. While most of DesignSpace's clients will purchase on-site, given the nature of the products and services, as well as price points, we still need to take all of our clients' purchasing preferences into account.

5. Finally, we have to make sure that we are measuring what is working and what is not. This can be difficult, given all the different stages of the customer journey. What particular messaging is effective? What particular format—or medium—is being used by clients when they make their final purchase decisions? We have to try and get our attributions and correlations as accurate as possible so we know how to invest our relatively limited marketing budget.

I looked up at Dave as I finished reading. "Okay, so the measurement you talk about in point five—how are we supposed to figure that out?"

"That's a good question. Most people, especially retailers, don't yet understand the extent to which digital will drive in-store transactions and how in-store visits affect online purchases. Most people view these sales channels individually or in silos, and underestimate the impact of their customers' digital expenditures on their total sales."

Dave moved to the white board and started drawing diagrams to illustrate his point. "It's important that we use the free measurement tools we have at our disposal today, software like Google Analytics, to determine online consumer behavior. But you also have to look at digital and in-store sales as a combined effort, especially when trying to understand your company's overall brand position and presence."

"Is Google Analytics powerful enough to tell us all we need to know about who's been visiting DesignSpace's website?"

"There are more powerful tools," Dave explained, "but the truth is, there is no one perfect measurement tool out there that will give us all the answers. We have to use a combination of information and assumptions to get at the truth, given the fact that somebody may have searched in-store, on their phone, on their tablet, or on a desktop, spoken to friends about a product or service, or done research on their preferred social network before deciding to buy."

I grimaced. "Joe's not going to be happy about that."

"If you think Joe's not going to be happy, wait until we talk to Raj about budget."

"Are you sure you guys are really friends?"

Dave laughed out loud. "Yes, absolutely," he said. "Now that I've told you a bit more about where and how we want to be found, let's talk about making this website mobile friendly."

I picked up my phone and started surfing through the DesignSpace website. *I could see it on my phone, but it wasn't very user-friendly; I had to keep zooming in and out just to read the text.*

"You've just discovered a major pet peeve for almost everyone who uses the Internet—which is pretty much everyone, or at least everyone DesignSpace might one day call a customer," Dave said as he watched me fuss with the text on my screen. "The need to zoom means the website isn't mobile friendly. There are a couple different lines of thought when it comes to mobile friendliness. The first is that if your website can't be easily read on a mobile device, then it's time to build a completely new one that's designed specifically for mobile. This is an interesting thought, and it's spurred the need for two separate, real-life implementations. For Android and Apple devices, people are developing apps that are specific to their store or brand. I would recommend this strategy for every business, particularly B2C companies, but even a firm like DesignSpace can benefit. That's because it creates the best possible user experience on that particular device for clients."

"But," I interrupted, "I heard a statistic that most apps get downloaded once, but are never opened again."

"You're right," Dave agreed. "Which brings us to the second option. There's been an evolution in website design where it's possible to detect exactly what kind of device is searching for the website, then deliver an optimized experience based on the screen size of that device. This is what I would recommend for DesignSpace. It's called a responsive website, and it responds to the device that's being used to explore the website, or, more specifically, the browser that's being used to navigate to that website."

"That makes sense. So, I'm guessing you just take the existing website and translate it to suit all these different devices?"

Dave shook his head. "Unfortunately, the technology isn't quite there yet. That means that at least for now, you have to do some tweaking to make sure your website's mobile appearance delivers the experience that your end users expect. When you're rebuilding the DesignSpace website, you have to bear in mind that people have screens that are massive—up to and including television monitors that are fifty or sixty inches wide—all the way down to a smartphone that's basically two inches by four inches wide. It's hard to optimize for all of these different screen sizes, so it's important to keep those fundamental considerations in mind as we're going through this process."

I looked at him and cocked my eyebrow. "*We're* going through it?"

"You didn't think I was going to let you handle this whole process alone, did you? Don't worry, I'm here to help. But we also have to consider the value of creating a mobile app for DesignSpace. Apps are now an integral part of most peoples' routines, and they're an excellent way to deepen relationships with customers. One of the most intriguing functions of an app is that you can use different notification settings to boost engagement and to develop loyalty by adding value for your customers."

"But aren't apps expensive to develop?" I asked.

"A basic app can cost anywhere from $20,000 to $40,000 to develop, so for some companies it can be a cost-prohibitive exercise. But if you need a unique way to communicate with customers, provide discounts, or even offer coupons toward a future purchase, apps are a great tool. They're also useful for delivering exclusive content in an environment that you control, while notifying customers about new features or other offers in your product line."

"But what happens when mobile is a larger percentage of a company's search? How do we position DesignSpace to take advantage of that?"

"Let's try to keep three points in mind," Dave said.

"First, we have to anticipate and be there for our customers when they're looking for us. And that means being mobile friendly. You have to remember that most clients aren't committed to a particular brand. They're looking for a solution to a problem. The real opportunity with mobile is that it gives us a chance to attract competitors' clients, especially if their websites aren't mobile optimized. Ultimately, just showing up with a visible, easily navigated website gets us in the game.

"Second, we have to be useful and relevant to our clients in the moment they're looking for answers. We have to bear in mind that people don't really like the hard sell, and consumers will gravitate toward brands that offer smaller, bite-sized, mobile-friendly pieces of educational content. When producing that content, we need to keep a few questions in mind. What do clients want to learn about DesignSpace services? Do those clients want to visit the showroom, or interact online, or maybe have our sales reps visit their offices? What are clients doing with our products and services? Do we have any content that conveys our value propositions and competitive advantage, like maybe videos? And finally, where are clients buying DesignSpace products? Are we enabling them to be able to ask questions and even purchase in a way that suits their needs?

"And the last point—our mobile experience has to be fast, navigable, and deliver an experience that benefits our clients in some way. Speed is key because mobile devices are often utilized over wireless networks as opposed to Wi-Fi, which means the website has to be quick to load and easy to use. As part of that mobile journey, we want to eliminate as many steps as possible and try to anticipate the needs of our end users. By no means is it a perfect science, and it takes experimentation to get it right, but when you do, the results can be massive in terms of driving sales and building brand awareness."

"Got it," I said. *I understood what Dave was saying, but I also knew we had a huge amount of work ahead.*

"There's one other thing that we shouldn't forget," Dave added. "Joe will measure our success not only by website clicks, page impressions, or brand recognition, but by the bottom line. In other words, we need to help improve DesignSpace's profit margins. If we can prove that online is profitable, then he'll continue to invest, and that's good news for everybody."

"And it should also keep Raj happy, right?" I asked with a smile.

"You got it." He smiled back.

✓ Mobile has become a critical aspect of online search

✓ Producing strong content isn't good enough: People need to be given the right information or the right offer at the right time in the right location

✓ Showrooming is a major challenge for retailers. It's when consumers come into a brick-and-mortar store, look at a product and pick one they want, and then go online and buy it elsewhere for less

✓ Having a user- and mobile-friendly site as a first point of contact can help your company maximize profits and ensure your clients are happy with their purchase decision

✓ To determine an organization's overall brand position and presence, it's important to leverage digital tools such as Google Analytics, as well as digital and in-store sales data (where applicable)

✓ Websites that can't be easily read on mobile devices should be rebuilt

✓ Mobile experiences must be user friendly, relevant to clients at the moment they're looking for answers, interactive to enable clients to ask questions or make purchases, and be fast and navigable

Chapter 7

Our conversation carried on for another hour or so before Dave looked at his watch. "It's getting late. We should wrap up. I'm sure you want to get out of here."

"I was actually going to stay late and do some research on competitors, take a deeper look at our website, and really think about what else we can improve, beyond what we've discussed so far. I should have packed dinner for myself."

"I was going to be in the office late tonight, as well. What do you say we grab another bite—again, my treat for listening to me so patiently and managing not to fall asleep—and then dive back into it for another hour or so? But then I'm kicking you out of here myself. You shouldn't work so late. You just started this job, after all." I do appreciate a boss—or a consultant who outranks me, or whatever Dave is—who respects his employees' work-life balance. It's even better if he's willing to pick up the check again. I felt kind of bad about that for a minute, and then I reminded myself that he was wearing designer jeans, glasses, and shoes. I decided to assume that his company, AlterRank, was doing pretty well.

"Sounds good," I said.

I packed up my laptop and proceeded back to my desk to get organized before heading out. Just then, an email from Joe appeared with links to various websites. His message was brief:

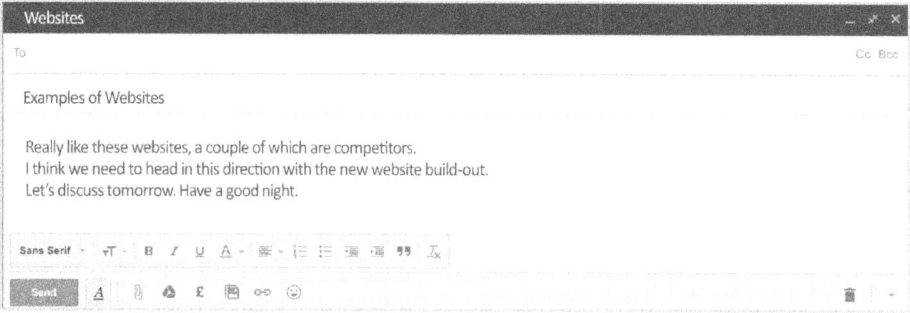

```
Websites                                                                    _ ⤢ ×

To                                                                      Cc  Bcc

Examples of Websites

Really like these websites, a couple of which are competitors.
I think we need to head in this direction with the new website build-out.
Let's discuss tomorrow. Have a good night.

Sans Serif  ·  ₸T ·  B  I  U  A ·  ≣ ·  ⋮≣  ≣  ⋰≣  ⋱≣  99  Iₓ

 Send      A   🖉   ⬥   £   🖼   ∞   ☺                          🗑    ·
```

Well, at least the links would give me an idea of Joe's preferences when it comes to website design.

I sent Helen a text letting her know that I'd be working late. That way, she'd know I was safe *and* that she wasn't missing out on any fun. I'd just hit Send when Dave appeared, wearing a beat up leather coat. "All set?"

"Yep, looks like it."

In came a reply from Helen.

Didn't you have lunch with him today, too? Do u have a thing for this guy? ;)

It was a typical Helen question to ask. I replied that no, I didn't date my bosses—especially married ones like Dave. That was in contrast to Helen, who'd gone on several dates with the CEO of her last company. Needless to say, it didn't end well.

Dave and I rode the elevator to street level and made our way outside. We walked five blocks to a street lined with trendy restaurants. The area was jammed with commuters heading home. We had to fight for sidewalk space.

Dave talked as we dodged fellow pedestrians. "I know we talked about it a bit at lunch, but tell me more about why you wanted to pursue a

113

marketing career. I've only been able to find tidbits of information about your background online."

Does this guy have a part-time job at the CIA or what, I wondered.

"Don't think I'm weird," he added. Great, now he really can read my thoughts. "I like to know as much as I can about the people I'm working with. It's one of my many professional quirks." No kidding.

"So far, I know that your interests are in design and marketing. And I know what you like to do in your free time, thanks your online posts, but I'd like to know more about your interests when it comes to business." *That fact that he was continuing to do research on me in his spare time still bothered me, but I couldn't exactly stop him, could I? Maybe if I just told him what he wanted to know . . .*

"To be honest, I wasn't really sure what I was going to do until I got partway through my bachelor's program and realized that I really enjoyed the giant puzzle that is marketing. I like the elements of psychology and business that are part of it, and the overall thrill of not quite knowing what will work or won't work. There's something really appealing about having to use your ingenuity and creativity to find solutions to help customers, often with little or no notice of challenges that are coming down the pipeline.

"At first, the old media formats struck me as a little bit boring, but once I got deeper into them, I realized the kind of creative juices it takes to develop a good TV spot, billboard, or radio ad that has the potential to stick in people's minds and make them interested in the product. Not that I've ever produced a commercial, of course, but it's interesting to have a broader sense of marketing and even know a little about advertising. I think that's all going to help me here."

Dave nodded, seemingly pleased that I was opening up a bit. "I got started in this field for some of the same reasons," he explained. "Back when I launched my career, the Internet hardly existed and we were at the tail end of using dial-up to connect. It was a really different experience to work in marketing. Everything has changed since then, even though certain fundamental considerations have remained pretty much the same."

We turned a corner and Dave motioned down the street. We had about ten restaurants to choose from in the next couple of blocks. "This may or may not be the case, but let's pretend you haven't been to any of these restaurants. I know I've only been to a couple. How do you suggest we decide which one might be the best bet?" he asked.

I'd been around Dave long enough in the few days I'd known him to understand that this wasn't just some random question. I was being tested. Luckily, I was a step ahead, having already taken out my phone to text my mom back with an update on how my day was progressing. It's very much like my mom to do regular checkups on her youngest daughter. *My older brother gets a call once every two weeks. Me, I get a call or text every day. I love her dearly, but sometimes I wish he and I could trade places.*

"Easy," I replied. "I'll look up some restaurants." I googled the name of the street, along with the search term *restaurants*. Only four of the ten eateries I could see came up on the search results page. I started scrolling through each, looking at different reviews from sites ranging from Yelp to Frommer's, as well as other third-party review platforms. I finally arrived at a review that I thought was the most helpful.

"That Italian place up there on the left has some good reviews and seems to have fairly prompt service. What do you say we try it out?"

I kept secret the fact that I was in the mood for penne arrabiata, my favorite pasta, and this just happened to be their signature dish.

Dave had a huge grin on his face. "Sounds good to me."

I looked at him curiously. "What's with the big smile?"

"What you just did is exactly what we want customers to do when they're looking for a company like DesignSpace. But let me ask: How did you make your decision? What were some of the influencing factors? Did you make up your mind or did Google and all of the third-party reviews help you come to this decision?"

"It was mostly the reviews," I said, trying to analyze my own thoughts, "but the fact that some of these little mom-and-pop shops don't even have a website certainly limits their opportunity to be discovered."

"Exactly," he said. "And the same applies to just about every business there is." Dave held the door open as we entered the tiny Italian restaurant. We were greeted by a friendly owner and, sure enough, were treated to prompt, friendly service—just as the reviews had promised. The place was called Abruzxos and, interestingly, it seemed as though they were trying to bridge the gap between the online and off-line worlds.

When we sat down at our table, I was shocked by the devices in front of us. Each place setting included the usual fork, knife, spoon, and glass-ware, but also an iPad. Once opened, the tablet had the usual collection of apps, as well as one specific to the restaurant. I opened it and found a digital menu, complete with photos and descriptions of each dish, as well as ratings from publicly verified websites.

The server made his way to our table and was very helpful in show-ing us how to review items, even though their system seemed very us-er-friendly. He spent more time informing us about various dishes and why each was delicious, but without ever trying to upsell. Nothing makes me angrier than a server who tries to pad a bill by pushing lobster or filet mignon on unwitting guests.

We were given the option of ordering electronically, so I ordered the penne dish and was given an estimated time for its arrival. I could have ordered for Dave or anyone else if we had more people at our ta-ble, then paid using my credit card. I'd heard of restaurants like this, but seeing this kind of technology in use at a little hole-in-the-wall trattoria was definitely surprising—and pretty cool.

Dave and I ate and talked about his kids and how he loved being a hockey dad, even though he hated the cost of outfitting his kids to play.

On our way out, after Dave settled the bill, the owner asked us if we had a good meal and a good experience. We gave an enthusiastic "yes," and he asked us to drop a quick review on Yelp or Google+ in exchange for a 10 percent discount coupon for our next visit. I pulled out my phone and obliged with a few glowing words about our meal and how I'd definitely be back. The owner handed me a discount coupon and offered a huge "thank you" before inviting us back.

"Wow, that's what I call service," I said to Dave as we ventured back into the chilly late-autumn night. "I guess my review surfing paid off."

As we were walking down the street, a dark sedan pulled up to an office building up ahead. A busy-looking businesswoman, probably some high-powered executive, got out of the back of the car, speaking on her smartphone. The vehicle looked like a cab, but there was no sign on the roof. Dave motioned for me to stop and watch the woman. She stood next to the car for a minute, typed a couple of notes on her phone, then walked into the building. The car remained in front of the building for a few more seconds while the driver also typed something into his phone. Then the car pulled away from the curb and rejoined traffic.

It all seemed pretty unremarkable. As we started walking again, I asked Dave why he'd wanted me to observe a businesswoman whom I didn't know doing something as commonplace as using a smartphone.

"You've heard of Uber, right?" Dave asked.

"Of course," I answered. "It's the car service that all the cab companies hate."

Dave smiled. "Yes, that's the one. What we were just watching was an Uber passenger rating a driver, and, most important, the driver rating the passenger. Trust-building is a two-way street in our hyper-connected world. It's now about Uber passengers rating drivers, and those same drivers rating their passengers. It's a feedback-on-feedback cycle, and it's quickly changing the very nature of commerce. It's an incredibly disruptive process and, to be honest, I think it will either transform or create entirely new industries in the years to come. Uber and its spin-offs like UberEATS— which is basically just Uber for food delivery—as well as services like Airbnb, are posing a major threat to traditional, entrenched business models."

All I could do was nod as I processed what that all meant. I knew about all of these new services, but I hadn't really considered their place in the larger economy. *Could these new start-ups change everything to the point where marketers like me don't have jobs anymore?* If that day ever comes, I guess it's back to the Bean for me—unless they come out with UberCoffee, too.

Dave kept talking as my mind drifted off into how this brave new world could manifest itself. "As a driver, I'd want to know what kind of passenger I'm picking up, and as a passenger, I'd want to keep my rating high so I get chosen over other potential passengers in busy times," he explained. "Of course, there are other companies that do the same thing. Upwork is an online marketplace for freelancers that offers digital services such as virtual assistance and graphic design. It's built on a similar feedback system to the one that powers services like Uber."

Dave recounted the story of a friend of his named Mauro who was doing some consulting for a local municipal transportation provider. Mauro was invited to a meeting with the transit company's president and CEO, senior vice-president, CIO, and the rest of the important bigwigs at the municipality. He asked Dave to come along and provide his consulting expertise in case they had any digital-specific questions. The mayor ended an important conference call with local business leaders just to be part of this particular discussion group, which was looking at ways to maximize local transit revenue over a two-year period.

Mauro was asked how technology innovation could impact the transit company's business over the next ten years. Dave explained that his friend was a twenty-five-year tech sector veteran who had seen entire industries grow from nothing to multibillion dollar corporations in just a couple of years with one well-timed initial public offering. Mauro threw out names like Twitter, Facebook, Google, even Apple—then outlined how they either hadn't existed or were relatively weak (as in the case of Apple) when he started out in the business. And now, we couldn't imagine a world without them.

As Dave recalled, Mauro leaned back in his chair and grinned. "It's going to completely disrupt your current model," Mauro told the transit stakeholders.

The executives looked at each other and back at him. "What do you mean when you use the word *disrupt*?" the CEO asked.

"Well, look at the technology that Uber has and how they're servicing people," Mauro began. "This is the future. Nowadays, the customer experience is everything, and in many cases, the experience with a service like Uber is better than the service with a traditional transportation model. The mind-blowing part of their model is they don't even own their own fleet of cars. They own an algorithm and an app. That's about it. The future isn't going to be about building railroads or other physical infrastructure where people have to come to a central station, then get on the bus or the train, take it into work, and then hail a cab to get to their office building."

At this point, according to Dave, the executives were absolutely enthralled and hanging on Mauro's every word.

"In the future, which in many cases is now, you'll be in your house and a vehicle will pull up to your driveway. It will honk or send a text message to your phone or whatever device you have. Then you'll go outside, where a self-driving vehicle will be waiting to take you exactly where you need to go. Your account will be automatically debited. You'll never put your hand in your pocket; you won't need to, because there won't be a driver to pay. You'll receive a customized ride that's on time, clean, and safe. Oh, and the vehicle will probably be powered by electricity."

This Mauro guy seemed pretty convincing. I think I would have been listening, too, if I'd been there.

"The guys looked at Mauro—and remember, these are people managing billions of dollars of traditional infrastructure and capital like buses and trains," Dave said, increasingly excited as he remembered the exact moment. "And they looked at him as if he had two heads. But then they were silent for a while. It was one of those moments in a corporate boardroom setting where everyone knows they should be saying something, but they were all at a loss for words. Finally—finally—the CEO looks up from his notepad and says, 'It looks like we have some thinking to do.'

"Mauro shrugged. 'It's up to you. If you want to be ahead of the curve, you can act now. Or, if you're simply satisfied in going along for the ride as this new wave of innovation crashes over you and your ridership takes a nosedive, you can wake up one day twenty years from now and realize that your transit service is completely obsolete. Don't get me wrong—there will always be a place for mass transportation in any major city, but you need to understand that the competition isn't what it used to be. You can't think in a box and just hope these new innovations will somehow disappear. Your business model is being threatened in a major way. And companies like Uber don't care about your legislated transit monopolies or taxi licensing regimes. They'll follow the law as necessary, sure, but consumers want these services and the smart people at Uber know it. They also understand that they can wait out politicians and keep lobbying for change. They will eventually win.'"

"You know what he does next?" Dave asked rhetorically, looking ready to burst.

"Um, no."

"He says to these people, 'If you don't have any more questions, I'm off to my next meeting.' Mauro gets up, shakes a couple of hands—everyone's looking at him in stunned silence—and leaves the meeting about thirty minutes early. It was the boardroom equivalent of a mic-drop moment. I followed him out the door because I wasn't sure what to do. I also thought it was the most bad-ass thing I'd ever seen."

At this point, Dave was almost giddy that a fellow tech nerd had had the stones to do such a thing.

"I'll be honest," he added, getting himself under control. "I would never do the same thing myself, but the executives must have liked something Mauro had to say. They hired him on a very lucrative consulting contract for the next two years to help modernize their transit system."

We had reached the office by this point, and met up with Joe in the reception area. He stopped for a chat. He was working late too, it seemed, and was apparently quite curious about how things were progressing on the marketing front.

"Working dinner?" he asked. "I appreciate you both staying late to keep the website-redesign ball rolling. This project means a lot to DesignSpace, and to me, of course."

"We had an interesting conversation about disruptive technologies and about what attracted us to marketing," I replied.

Joe laughed. "I hope he didn't put you to sleep with his stories of the pre-Internet glory years."

"I don't think I did," Dave said with a smile. "She didn't go face-down in her appetizer at any point in the conversation, so she seemed to be fairly engaged. But thanks for pointing out that I'm apparently the most boring human alive."

"Your words, not mine—because I would never say that," Joe ribbed Dave.

"In fact, it sounds like Susan might have even gained a few insights that will help her breathe new life into the DesignSpace website." My cue to impress the boss.

"There are a number of things we're going to need to do to bring your website up to par," I said with as much assurance as I could muster, "starting with driving increased traffic."

"You mean *our* website," Joe corrected with a grin. My stomach twisted into an uncomfortable knot. *Had I said the wrong thing, or given the impression that I wasn't in it for the long haul?*

"And it's not just about driving traffic," he continued. "Don't forget that one of our main goals is boosting company-wide revenue to help pay for all of the fancy furniture and technology that fills this place and empowers us to serve our clientele. But I'm sure you were just about to say that, right?"

I nodded and took a deep gulp of air, which I'm sure they could hear. Joe's message was clear: *the website had to be a revenue generator for DesignSpace, or else don't even bother redesigning it.*

"No problem." I tried to put my ill-timed gulp behind me and recapture my earlier assurance. "I'm in good hands with Dave here. We'll get things sorted out and get your website metrics back on track."

Joe nodded his approval. "I'll leave you to it—and I look forward to hearing your suggested changes."

With that, Joe made his way back into his office and immediately picked up the phone.

Dave and I walked down the hall to the boardroom and eased back into our familiar surroundings.

I opened my computer again and looked at the DesignSpace website with everything I'd learned at dinner in mind. There are numerous disruptive technologies that are shaking up businesses—including this one—all over the world. Earlier in the day, I noticed that one of our competitors had an incredible app and a highly interactive website. Their office designers are also available online 24/7. I had no idea how they managed to deliver that kind of high-touch level of service, but it seemed to be working. They were number two in the industry, and had just a handful more employees than DesignSpace.

But the big question: *How on Earth was I supposed to get this website to generate the kind of revenue that Joe wants?* I must have mumbled that last part out loud, because Dave smiled and told me not to worry; we'd start at the beginning and rebuild it piece by piece if necessary.

I looked at the existing site, practically in desperation. "But this thing is almost beyond salvage," I said. "It doesn't really serve its purpose and it doesn't show up well on my phone. I have to zoom and scroll around just to read some of the text that's there."

Dave offered a sympathetic look. "Yes, having a responsive website is very important. But like I said, let's start at the beginning."

"First," Dave started, "Joe has given us a very clear indication as to what he wants the website to eventually do. And that's a good thing. He wants to generate revenue for DesignSpace and turn his site into his best and most profitable sales person. Most of my clients only have a vague notion of how they want their websites to look and feel. I can't tell you how frustrating that can be. It's really important that companies have a strategic vision for all of their digital properties, be they websites or apps, before they start building them out. Otherwise, you can get halfway through the process and realize you've gone in the wrong direction. That ends up wasting a lot of time and money."

Dave stood up, walked over to the whiteboard, and picked up a dry-erase marker.

"Let me ask you a question," he said. "Do you think the DesignSpace website has a traffic problem, or a conversion problem?"

I looked down at the website, which was open on my laptop, and took a moment to consider my answer.

"I'd say both," I replied. "The site doesn't get much traffic, but the traffic it does get doesn't convert."

"How do you know it doesn't get much traffic?" Dave asked.

"Mostly because Joe said he doesn't get many leads from it." It sounded like a pretty logical conclusion, or so I thought. "But that's a conversion issue, not necessarily a traffic issue," Dave said. "Why don't we find out for sure before we draw any conclusions?"

"Okay," I said. "But how exactly are we going to do that?"

"I installed Google Analytics on the site a month ago, when Joe first brought me into this discussion. So let's log into that program and see what we've got."

Dave walked around the table, quickly logged into Google and pulled up the analytics account for three of Joe's websites. I didn't know much about the other two, which belonged to his satellite companies, but I was quietly hoping I wouldn't have to work on those as well—or at least not until I was finished with DesignSpace's website.

I looked at the Google Analytics dashboard. I could see that the traffic on two of the sites was hovering at fewer than a thousand visitors per month, but one seemed to be doing much better, with almost thirty thousand visitors per month.

I asked the first and most obvious question that came to mind: "What's a good benchmark for traffic? Those two sites are registering pretty low in visits, but the other one is showing thirty times as many visitors."

"Good observation," said Dave. "And that was a pleasant surprise. To answer your question, the amount of traffic depends on the target niche you're looking at. A B2B website will have much less traffic than a breaking news site like Huffington Post, and rightfully so. That's because in the case of the former, you're basically looking to attract existing or potential clients, which is an infinitesimally smaller audience than the entire general population that a news website is targeting. If we could attract HuffPo numbers, Joe wouldn't just be happy—he'd probably rename the company after you. In other words, traffic benchmarking really depends on the purpose of the site, and the specific goal that it's attempting to accomplish. Remember our conversation about landing pages and how they're built?"

"Sure," I answered.

"Now we should take a more holistic approach, taking into account the entire website. So let's look at one of the low traffic sites—which happens to be DesignSpace, and the one Joe wants us to start with. We'll come back to his other websites later."

"*Start*?" I blurted out.

"Sorry, didn't he mention that if you do a great job with DesignSpace he wants you to work on his other sites, as well?" *Well that answers that question, I suppose!*

"The risks and rewards of redesigning a website start with the main content of the website," Dave began. "The main content is the reason the website exists. It should support the key value propositions and strategy of the website, as well as providing an exceptional user experience to its end users. We don't have to blow the budget on developing a super-advanced website from scratch, but we do need to invest some significant time to thinking through how the site should be presented, the content that's going to go on it, and how we can best show off the experience and skill that

DesignSpace has within these walls."

Hopefully, that includes someone equipped to do my job, I thought, wishing I could laugh out loud at the wittiness of my inner sarcasm.

"Secondary to that is supplementary content," Dave continued. "This is additional content on any particular page that will help with the overall user experience. Supplementary content can be content that's found on the website itself, or provided by a link to other content off the website. As a general rule of thumb, though, you want people to stay on your website for as long as possible so you can persuade them that you're the expert and authority on the subject. You can do this through features designed to help shoppers find products other than the ones you're suggesting, for example, or those that other people have purchased. Those are just two examples of good supplementary content."

I was taking notes on my laptop, knowing full well that at any moment Dave would probably send me these points by email.

After another hour or so of discussion, Dave looked down at his laptop. "Is it 8:30 already? I'm so sorry to have kept you this late. You need to get out of here. We can pick this up tomorrow."

"You're not keeping me, I want to get up to speed and be sure that I know what I'm doing. We also need to set a strategy to get this website redesigned."

Dave cracked a slight smile as he packed his laptop. "I like the way you think, and I love your commitment, but I also believe in people having the time they need to rest and recharge their batteries—and it looks like that time is now."

Dave grabbed his coat and draped it over his arm as he picked up his bag. "I'll see you tomorrow."

And with that, our very long day came to an end.

✓ Many websites face traffic or conversion challenges, and sometimes both simultaneously

✓ Traffic benchmarking is dependent on the purpose of the website, and the specific goal that it's attempting to accomplish

✓ The main content of a website should promote your company's key value propositions, as well as providing an exceptional user experience to its end users

✓ Supplementary content is additional content on any particular page that will help improve the overall user experience. It can be found on the website itself, or provided by a link to content off the website

Chapter 8

I woke up the next morning with an extra spring in my step.

For the first time in years—okay, probably forever—I was really excited to get to work. I raced through my usual shower-breakfast-Bean-bus ritual and practically floated into the office. I was finally satisfied with the work I was doing and felt I was on the right track in my career. Most importantly, I was ready to rise to the challenges ahead.

Not surprisingly, Dave was already waiting for me in the boardroom, despite the fact that I arrived fifteen minutes early.

"What am I going to have to do to beat you into the office?" I asked with a teasing grin.

"Probably start your day at 5 a.m., like I do," he said. "Don't mind me, I'm strange that way. I wake up, work out, and get to work early so I can get home and spend some quality time with the family before bed. I've been working longer days lately to move this project forward, but this is a bit unusual even by my standards."

I set my laptop on the table next to my coffee and got ready for another long day of learning.

Dave leaned forward in his chair. "Are you ready to talk about some ways we can prove value to Joe and Raj?"

I nodded. "I've been a little bit concerned about that, given everything you've told me about how some aspects of digital marketing can be difficult to quantify."

"The first thing you have to understand is that building the sexiest website possible is not a guarantee of success. What we have to do instead is start by figuring out the real purpose of the website. Then we can use measurement tools like Google Analytics to measure its success or failure."

"Okay," I said, "but we don't want it to look like crap, right?"

Dave could only laugh at my question. "Absolutely not, and that's why we have to figure a few things out."

Within seconds, he'd emailed me yet another list of points.

Cheat Sheet – Key Questions to Consider When Developing a Website Strategy

1. What are the business objectives for the website?

2. What are some very specific, measurable goals we can use to determine success or failure?

3. What are the key performance indicators (KPIs)? We have to make sure we get agreement on these and set targets for each.

4. Which behavioral outcomes need to be analyzed to understand if we've succeeded or failed?

"Sounds pretty simple," I said, once I was finished reading.

"Not too difficult, is it?" Dave replied. "That said, we can break it down into a further three steps."

I kept the cheat sheet open on my laptop and added to it as Dave continued to speak.

Cheat Sheet, continued

1. How are we acquiring traffic? Are we using all three available online channels—our earned, owned, and paid traffic (more about this later)? Are we maximizing each channel?

2. When we're measuring behavior, what behavior do we want website visitors to exhibit? What pages do we want them to see? What actions should they take? What experience is the ultimate one for the customer to perform our desired actions?

3. Strong outcomes are what we're driving toward, but are any in particular positively impacting DesignSpace's bottom line? Are we looking to drive online purchases or phone calls by prospective clients? Are we looking to generate a qualified online lead, or have a customer sign up for an email? What exactly are we trying to do?

Dave waited for me to finish keying my notes before he spoke again. "Let's see if we can steal some of Joe's time and get answers to these business objective–focused questions." Together, we walked down the hall to Joe's office. He was in the midst of typing something on his laptop when Dave knocked on the door.

"Hey Joe, can we borrow you for a few minutes?" he asked.

Joe looked up from his computer. "Sure, let me just finish this email and I'll be right with you. Have a seat."

Dave and I walked into his office and sat in the two very comfortable—and likely expensive—leather couches as he finished typing.

"So, what's up?" Joe asked, once the familiar *whoosh* indicated sent mail had sounded.

"Still on track to make magic happen," Dave said, drastically overselling our work thus far. "Susan is still an excellent learner and I'm still here, so that's something."

"That's always a bonus," Joe replied dryly.

"Dave is doing a pretty decent job of explaining the logic behind a lot of what I see on a day-to-day basis. I have a feeling I'm never going to look at the Internet in the same way again," I added.

Joe laughed. "That's a good thing. So, what can I do for you?"

Dave took the lead. "We need to understand a few different things about your website in order to effectively design and implement a strategy for you. You and I had some discussions early on in this process, but Susan wasn't a part of them, so I figured this would be a good time to bring her up to speed and define exactly what our business objectives are for the site."

"Perfect," Joe said. "Ask away."

Dave looked to make sure I had my laptop ready to take notes, which I did.

"While the first and most difficult question is '*Why does this website exist?*'" Dave began, "we also want to know why we're going down this road and completing this project. But before you answer those questions, let me provide some possible answers."

Dave read a numbered list of four items off of his own laptop. I quickly added the notes to my growing cheat sheet. He called them the four C's:

CheatSheet, continued

Is our objective to:

1. Contact – create awareness,

2. Consider – have the customer consider our offering versus others,

3. Convert - generate leads or sales, or

4. Care – keep in touch with existing customers, highlighting events and/or supply information.

I glanced up to see a slightly perplexed look on Joe's face. "I thought I made it clear yesterday that this project is all about generating leads and driving sales to fuel our bottom-line growth," he said. "Nothing has changed since then."

"Perfect," Dave answered, ignoring the frustration in Joe's voice. "But what about creating awareness for your brand or engaging with the community? Aren't those important, too?"

Joe considered this for a moment before answering. "Yes, and we're doing a lot of other advertising, so having an online message that supports our print and off-line advertising makes sense."

"And what about your showroom?" Dave asked. "I know DesignSpace's clients are generally companies ranging from well-funded start-ups to large corporations, but doesn't it make sense to engage with the local community as well?"

Joe nodded a definitive yes, but not before pointing out his budget limitations.

"Don't worry, I get it," Dave reassured him. "Now we can narrow those goals down into measurable action steps we can take on the website. Let's start with generating leads. I know you have some great salespeople here, so what information do you need to capture in order for them to follow up with potential leads?"

"You can talk to Steve in sales about this, but I think email and phone contact information would be the most important."

Dave nodded. "Gotcha. So that would mean including some kind of a form to fill out. To get customers to take action, we usually need content that will entice them to learn more about your products and services. Do you have anything like that?"

"Sure," said Joe. "We've got lots of stuff that we developed for new product lines. Steve can get that to you too."

Dave glanced in my direction before speaking again. "What we'll do is create content that can only be downloaded after the submission of contact information," he said, turning his attention back to Joe. "I'm curious about something else. How much is a lead worth to you?"

Joe looked at Dave and raised his eyebrow. "Are you charging by the lead now?" he asked as he picked up the phone on his desk and keyed in a number. He waited for the person on the other and to answer, and then asked them to join us. Five seconds later, Steve showed up at the door. "Dave is looking for some answers about our sales infrastructure and strategy," Joe explained. "By the way, this is Susan, our new marketing person. I don't think you two have met."

We shook hands and Steve turned to Dave. "What do you need to know?"

"I just have a couple of quick questions about how much a lead would be worth to you and the sales team," Dave said. "Off the top of your head, do you know the conversion rate for incoming leads?"

"Our conversion rate for outbound sales is approximately 1 percent," Steve replied. "If we call a hundred people, we get maybe three appointments, and maybe one of those appointments will convert to a sale. Inbound it's probably in the 2 to 5 percent range, but currently we don't get too many inbound leads."

"We're working on that." Dave grinned. "Tell me, what's the average size of the orders for the leads you do manage to convert?"

"Our average order is about $45,000," Steve said, "but some are much larger, of course. It really depends on the client and the amount of furniture or type of design services they need to purchase at a given time."

This was all good information, but Dave wasn't done yet. "And approximately how many repeat customers do you have? Let's continue to ballpark these numbers. How much revenue do you get per customer over the entire lifetime of their engagement with DesignSpace?"

Steve thought for a second. "I'd say most companies order from us, on average, about three or four times in their lifespan as a DesignSpace customer."

"Would it be safe to say the average lifetime value of a customer is about $150,000?"

Steve nodded. "I think that would be fair."

"And how much profit do you make on each order?" Dave asked.

Joe piped up—clearly this part of the discussion meant the most to him. "Our profit margin is approximately 40 percent," he said.

"Okay, so that works out to approximately $60,000 per customer over their lifetime involvement with the company. Perfect. Thanks, Steve."

Steve looked at me and then at Joe. "Anything else?"

Joe shook his head. "Nope, that's it, thanks. I appreciate the time."

As Steve left the office, Joe asked if we had all the information we needed to proceed.

Dave chuckled. "It's definitely a good starting point. The next thing we need from you is a sense of how much you want to spend. Then we can come back to you with a proposal."

"If I'm making money on every single inquiry that comes in, the budget is unlimited!" Joe said. He was laughing, but I could tell he wasn't entirely kidding.

"Of course it is," Dave responded, "but the real issue is how much money you're willing to budget and put out there in the real world. Once we know that, we can work on ensuring that you're making money on each lead we generate."

"Why don't you come back to me with a couple of different proposals," Joe suggested, "and I'll see where I can find some money to budget for the initiative. I have a rough figure in mind, but I want to hear your ideas before making a decision."

"No problem." Dave nodded as he stood up to leave the room. I followed close behind. Back to the boardroom, Dave sat down in his chair. "Did you find that conversation helpful?" he asked.

"I think it certainly gives us a starting point, as you said, but why were you so interested in the profitability and average order size tied to each customer?"

"We're going to be using those metrics to determine the cost per lead that Joe can afford to sustain over the long term. Then we can find the best solutions possible for him to maximize his return on investment," Dave explained.

"Makes sense," I said, "but he didn't really give you a budget to work with, so where do we start?"

"We start by breaking this all down into bite-sized chunks so that Joe can make decisions with a bit more certainty and clarity. And we give him a couple of different scenarios that he can respond to," he added, gesturing for me to open up my laptop so I could keep taking notes.

"First and foremost, we've been discussing rebuilding his website. Speaking in general terms, let's say Joe has a budget of $2,000 per month. That will give him a total budget of $24,000 per year. Given the cost of web development these days and the timeline needed, we can safely allocate $10,000 and three months to develop a website." He paused, then asked a question. "

But what happens if, after those three months with a new website, he decides he only has $1,000 a month to spend? What are some of the next steps we should be ready to carry out?"

Beats me, I thought.

"In that scenario, the first thing we should do is evaluate the options for that $1,000-per-month spend. There are lots strategies and tactics to choose from, but we have to keep Joe's long-term business objectives and customer cost-of-acquisition goals in mind—specifically, what he's willing to spend to generate new leads."

Funny, my inner voice said, *my long-term goal is to avoid getting fired—which is a much more modest goal than Joe's plans to dramatically grow his business!*

"There are three basic types of traffic that will come to your website," Dave said, slipping back into teaching mode. "These are your paid, owned, and earned visitors. Let's start by exploring the differences." I started taking notes again.

"Your owned property is your website. Your website is really the only thing you have full control over on the Internet. The other two types of traffic are: Your paid traffic, where you rent visitors to your website by paying other websites to direct traffic your way and your earned traffic from other websites, which can change their policies and procedures at any time. Fans and followers on Facebook and YouTube are examples here. You have to be very careful how, and in what ways, you invest in those properties.

These websites direct traffic your way in the form of likes, fans, followers, or referral traffic. This is great free traffic, and tends to come after your website is established and your brand name has been built up over a long period of time."

Dave sprang to his feet and started pacing. He was getting into the groove again.

"Going back to your paid traffic. This traffic tends to come mostly from Google Ad Words, Facebook ads, Twitter Cards, or other paid means of driving traffic to your website. Paid traffic is usually derived from pay-per-click ads or from paying by the number of impressions you receive on a particular website. That's why I also think of it as rented traffic. As soon as you stop paying rent, the traffic stops coming to your site."

I was typing feverishly at this point, hoping for an email from Dave chock full of notes to relieve me of my duties.

"Sorry, I don't have notes to email you for this one," he said.

This is not my lucky day.

Dave took a breath and let me catch up with my notes. When I indicated I was ready, he continued. "I much prefer the pay-per-click model for companies like DesignSpace, which is driving toward specific revenue goals. You can measure how much each click costs you and how many clicks it takes to convert someone to a customer, and then see if the math makes sense."

"So, if we rebuild the DesignSpace website and then spend money after that, the question really revolves around the best use of the $1,000, correct?" I asked, to make sure I was following.

"Exactly," Dave said. "For most companies, a multi-part strategy makes sense. You always want to be found organically on Google, and not have to pay for each click forever. Free clicks are the best kind of traffic, but since we're developing a website that's going to be competing with websites that have been around forever, this is a major uphill battle."

I looked up at him. "You're suggesting that we try a paid strategy first to drive traffic?"

"Unfortunately, with only $1,000 per month, we don't really have enough budget to conduct an effective paid strategy. There are companies in the same space as us that are spending that kind of money PER DAY with their pay-per-click advertising. That budget per month is a drop in the bucket. If we were to take that money and try to compete with larger competitors in the field, we'd basically be throwing the budget away. That approach would also mean bringing in a specialist to help us manage a campaign, and those specialists usually charge in the range of $1,000 to $5000 per month, if not more. With a modest budget like ours, a paid campaign isn't really an option."

I must have looked disappointed.

"Don't worry, all is not lost," Dave said, offering an encouraging smile. "What we need to do is start building the foundation of Joe's search engine optimization strategy to try to get some organic traffic. A budget of $1,000 per month is enough to launch a good SEO-focused content strategy.

"But first thing's first. Building the DesignSpace site is going to chew up the first $10,000. After that, we should spend some time doing some competitive analysis to create local demand for our products. There are a lot of potential customers within a ten-block radius of this office that we've never even tried to tap. We do that by optimizing DesignSpace's online presence for local searches. There are plenty of SEO companies out there that will happily take your money and do nothing with it. To do it better and cheaper, we need to remember that the key to any strong search-focused content strategy is to make sure you're getting links from good, authoritative sites and are generating content on your site that's actually useful, helpful, and potentially entertaining to your target market."

"I think that makes sense," I said.

"This $1,000 per month budget will build the foundation for the additional budget expenditure after the fact, like on content development or other online marketing initiatives, for example. So we have to make sure that Joe is set up with his Google local listing, as well as Apple maps and all the local directories, not to mention all of the important social networks. We have to have a profile and cover page, and make sure that DesignSpace information is consistent across all properties."

I gave him a skeptical look. "Why would you want to be featured in all of those places if we don't have the budget to support any activity on those networks?"

"I see your point. The problem is you don't know exactly where a customer or a prospect might be looking for you. They may use Facebook on a daily basis and expect you to be there, for example. Realistically, everybody knows that Facebook is a social network platform, and businesses that try to market to people on Facebook—but do it poorly—are frowned upon. But everyone who is on those social networks expects businesses to be found there. All you have to do with your profile is have a line that says, *For more information, please check out our website,* and then provide a link they can click on."

"Got it."

"We'll probably use the fourth or fifth months' budget to get all of the relevant information, photos, creative, and other necessary elements prepared. Once we have our presence established and the website up and running, we can budget for our long-term growth by investing in a detailed SEO strategy."

"We have to make sure that any strategy we undertake has the end user in mind. When designing these pages, we have to remember that they want to know, they want to go, or they want to buy something when on this website."

"I remember you mentioning that, but in a slightly different way before," I noted, thinking that my head might explode if I heard Dave drive home the same, albeit important, message again.

"The key to Google friendliness and to the success of this website re-development project is to not think of our website as a book. This is a very common mistake. Google sees your website as a collection of pages, not a book that reads from start to finish. Google's search algorithm is far more sophisticated and granular than that. It wants to find the right answer to your question, every time. If we can figure out the main questions that our customers are asking, and then design pages in response to those queries and to address the needs of those particular users, Google will reward us by serving our page higher in the search results."

"If I'm understanding this correctly, our next step after the preparation of the creative elements is to write web pages that answer questions, correct?"

"Absolutely. The remainder of our budget will be allocated to content generation and link-building for our SEO efforts."

"Got it," I said. "What's next?"

"Well, what's next is we ask Joe for more budget." He chuckled. "Or, should I say, we ask Raj for more budget."

"Good luck with that," I replied.

"Sorry, but that's actually your job, not mine! What we have to do now is build the case for a budget ten times the one Joe is allotting, or $10,000 per month. Let's assume that the budget will grow over time. We have to wait until the website is complete before we can start the SEO portion of the process. The budget will still be $1,000 a month for the first three months, and then another $1,000 or $2,000 to bolster our online presence through content creation. Once you have the website up, the additional budget can go toward SEO efforts, as well as a paid-traffic campaign.

"I would recommend developing a content and white paper/resource-generation plan for Joe. This content and information will position the company as a thought leader. It can also help sales acquire new customers by nudging them to register in order to download content. Our goal is to get leads that Steven and the sales team can close. The more valuable information we put out there for free, maybe with teasers to exceptionally valuable information or exclusive content, the better for building a strong community with plenty of sales leads."

I paused for a second. "That sounds expensive."

"I would budget roughly $2,000 per month for that portion of the strategy. Where does that leave us in terms of the total budget?"

I scanned my notes and started to add the figures. "We've allotted $1,000 for social and $2,000 for a content strategy. That still leaves us with about $7,000 a month to spend."

"This is where our discussion with Steve comes into play. We'll have to spend some of the budget on developing specific landing pages for paid efforts so that we can track them. Let's allocate another $500 or $1,000 per month for testing and optimizing each page. Oh, and we would start off with a specific number of campaigns with specific revenue goals. If we're going to be running, say, four campaigns, that will cost in the neighborhood of $2,000 or so a month. So now our total monthly budget spend is at about $5,000.

"Given the fact that the average lifetime value of any particular customer is $60,000 in profit, we have to make sure that each customer is acquired profitably. Joe's tolerance for this will depend on his goals—specifically whether he's trying to grow the business and maintain profitability as he grows, or whether he's just trying to maintain his current customer base, or whether he is willing to grow without a profit. Because we know in this case that he's trying to grow, we could probably safely dedicate 50 percent of this lifetime value to acquiring new customers. This gives us about $1,000 to spend to acquire a $2,000 lead."

I analyzed my notes again. "To clarify, you're saying we have about $5,000 per month to spend on acquiring new customers through paid channels?"

"That's right," Dave nodded. "But don't forget, we're going to need to have someone on board to manage these channels, and their services may cost about 15 percent of our total spend, so we actually have a bit more than $4,000 of real advertising dollars to spend."

"Theoretically then, with $4,000 to spend, we should expect to acquire four new leads."

"Yes, at the very least. Ideally, it would be better if we could acquire them for less, but that gives us our goal and allows us to present coherent budget figures so Joe can make his decision. If we have optimized landing pages that we're spending about $2,000 on, plus the actual paid search that we're spending another $5,000 to stage, then technically, we should be acquiring seven new leads for that $4,000 budget."

"I guess this is why we need professional help in acquiring these customers, right?"

"Exactly," said Dave. "We want to make sure our budget is utilized in the most effective way possible."

	JAN	FEB	MAR	APR	MAY	JUN	JUL	AUG	SEPT	OCT	NOV	DEC	TOTAL
BUDGET	1,000	1,000	1,000	2,000	2,000	2,000	6,000	6,000	6,000	11,000	11,000	11,000	60,000
Expenses													
SEO	1,000	1,000	1,000	1,000	1,000	1,000	1,000	1,000	1,000	1,000	1,000	1,000	12,000
Social - Organic				1,000	1,000	1,000	1,000	1,000	1,000	1,000	1,000	1,000	9,000
Content - Generation							2,000	2,000	2,000	2,000	2,000	2,000	12,000
Conversion Rate Optimization							2,000	2,000	2,000	2,000	2,000	2,000	12,000
Paid Acquisition										4,000	4,000	4,000	12,000
Agency Fees										1,000	1,000	1,000	3,000
TOTAL	1,000	1,000	1,000	2,000	2,000	2,000	6,000	6,000	6,000	11,000	11,000	11,000	60,000

"So, what we want to do through our SEO efforts is to acquire three new customers, and through our paid efforts we need to acquire seven new customers per month with our total budget being $60,000."

"That's correct. And we have to present the case to Joe that, month after month, this is a worthwhile investment. The real key here is to track where our leads are coming from, and to shift budget around depending on what channel is the most successful. I haven't spoken too much about earned traffic, but that often comes as a result of the SEO efforts and brand-building campaigns on social media." On my laptop, I opened DesignSpace's Google Analytics results.

"This might be a dumb question," I began, "but can you find the different channels on Google Analytics?"

Dave walked around the table and leaned over my shoulder. He pointed at my screen. "On the left-hand side there's a sub-category called acquisition."

I pulled it up and reviewed the data results.

	Acquisition			Behavior			Conversions		
	Sessions	% New Sessions	New Users	Bounce Rate	Pages / Session	Avg. Session Duration	Ecommerce Conversion Rate	Transactions	Revenue
	104,983	82.64%	86,754	53.00%	3.75	00:02:01	1.18%	1,243	$181,620.13
1 Social	44,907			70.95%			<0.01%		
2 Organic Search	35,015			43.46%			0.95%		
3 Direct	10,600			46.30%			3.33%		
4 Referral	10,467			20.72%			4.69%		
5 Paid Search	2,087			34.79%			1.87%		
6 Affiliates	1,231			45.49%			0.08%		
7 Display	676			29.29%			1.48%		

"As you can see," Dave said, "in DesignSpace's case, there are seven main channels from which to acquire traffic. The first is organic search—plain old Google searches where you show up in the search results ranking and a user clicks on your page. The second is direct, which means the user typed *DesignSpace.com* into the search bar of their web browser.

"The third is referral traffic, which comes from other websites driving traffic to yours. That could be from an article about a company, for example, that includes a link to DesignSpace.

"The fourth type of traffic is social traffic, which refers to any users that come to your website from social websites.

"The fifth type of traffic is email traffic. If Joe sends out email blasts to attract prospects, any traffic that comes to the site as a result will, if tagged correctly, show up as email traffic.

"The sixth type of traffic is paid search traffic. If your Google Analytics account is linked to your Google Ad Words account, this will show you where all of the traffic is coming from and how it's converting.

"And the final category is 'other.' This is where Google throws in everything that doesn't neatly fit into one of the other six categories.

I was still trying to make sense of the Google Analytics dashboard.

"I notice that Joe has conversions set up on his account," I pointed out.

Dave smiled as he walked back around to the other side of the table. "And what do those conversions tell you about the different channels?" he asked.

I looked at the graph on my screen. "Some channels seem to have a higher conversion rate than others."

Dave nodded. "And?"

"It seems like his organic search traffic converts at a certain rate, while his email traffic converts at a much lower rate. At the same time, his paid search efforts convert at a much higher rate."

"That's exactly what they're supposed to do. Think about email for a moment. You could send out thousands of emails, but only 5 or 10 percent will get opened. And of those, only 5 or 10 percent of the readers will click on a link. Of *those*, only 5 or 10 percent will actually perform some kind of action on your page. The number can get quite small, quite quickly. The good thing about email is that it's cheap, so contacting lots of people will make sense as long as they've opted into your program." Dave paused to let that sink in, then asked another question.

"Now, tell me again, what's the conversion rate for paid search versus direct and organic searches?"

I looked over the data. "The direct search is converting at 2.1 percent, the organic search is converting at 4.2 percent, and the paid search is converting at 10.32 percent."

"That's a good thing," he noted. "When you think about it, your paid searches should always convert better than your organic and direct searches, because, technically speaking, you should only be driving targeted traffic from your paid search efforts. You can use organic search and direct search to figure out what people are looking for on your site, but you need to focus very closely on where your dollars are being spent when it comes to paid search."

I nodded in agreement.

"Let's consider a hypothetical scenario. What if you and I could talk Raj and Joe into spending $100,000 a month on a digital marketing plan? Where would you spend the money?"

My eyes opened a little bit wider. Probably a raise for myself, I thought. I didn't say that out loud. "I have no idea! Just the thought of that makes me a little uncomfortable."

"Look again at the numbers. You just gave me the answer."

"Well, the highest conversion rate is from paid search, so I guess a simple answer would be to spend more on paid search to get more conversions."

"Good. Using numbers to make a case and build a story is very important. Now, we don't have all the information that we need with this one screenshot alone. But your gut instinct is correct. We can use other tools, such as additional social media monitoring and marketing, but you have to make sure that we're targeting our prospective buyers across different and relevant locations and venues. We then have to figure out how much it costs us to acquire each customer through each channel, and whether or not each channel is profitable. Because even if paid search is converting at two and a half times the rate of organic search, organic search is free, and paid search isn't. So we have to be very careful about the percentage of our budget that we're using to acquire our traffic through these different channels. Then we have to boil it down to one particular metric, usually

CPA—cost per acquisition—or ROAS, which is return on ad spend. If we can break down the performance of all of our channels with one metric, we can evaluate them each on their own merits when comparing them to each other." My fingers were going numb.

"And how do we do that?" I asked while trying to type 300 words per minute.

Dave laughed. "Are you sure you're up for it? You've taken in a ton of information already today."

I gave him a look that said, "Bring it on."

"Okay then. The first thing we need to do is to review our earlier conversation with Steve to figure out how much it actually costs us to acquire each customer. Then we need to figure out how much money we make from an average customer over their lifetime. Again, this is called a lifetime value—or LTV.

"Say, for example, that a customer will purchase a new office chair from DesignSpace every five years, for a total of twenty-five years. If each office chair cost $300, we'd multiply that by five and the customer lifetime gross value is $1,500. If Joe makes a 60% profit on each purchase that means the lifetime profit value of a customer is $750. This is actually the more important metric, because you need to know how much profit you make before you know how much you can spend to acquire the customer."

I nodded to indicate my understanding, and Dave continued. "Let's say that Joe has to pay overhead and miscellaneous costs in the neighborhood of 30 percent of his gross profit. If I do some quick math, that amounts to $225. So Joe's real profit on this particular customer is $750 minus $225. That means this customer's lifetime value is $525."

This all seemed too logical. It was bound to get highly complicated at some point soon.

"Now, we both know that Joe is going to want to keep some of that money for himself, and he'll have to pay taxes on his profit, so let's assume he's comfortable with spending 50 percent of his $525 to acquire that customer. This gives us $262.50 for acquisition purposes. That is the absolute maximum that Joe will want to spend on any one channel, whether that be advertising on TV, radio or online, exhibiting at trade shows, or whatever. That is the one number that matters. That is the success rate against which all sales and marketing efforts should be measured."

I was still typing notes.

"And this is where we can actually get into trouble with sales people like Steve."

I looked up from screen. "Um, how?"

"We've just determined that DesignSpace's customer acquisition cost is $262.50. If our salespeople aren't generating new customers at that same cost or below, taking into account their salaries and bonuses and commissions, then we potentially need to make the case to change our acquisition strategy. That type of conclusion is likely going to annoy a salesperson like Steve, who's probably got his own way of doing things. But it also provides a good opportunity for sales and marketing to work well together, because having one metric to determine where to allocate resources is the best way to make that decision, assuming that the number is accurate. If, for example, it makes more sense to use paid search at $100,000 a month as opposed to hiring fifteen new salespeople, then that's the business case we'd have to present to Joe."

I focused on my keyboard, trying to hide the grimace on my face. *That was a pretty cold assessment. Was Dave seriously suggesting that our job was to make an argument for either retaining or firing people? Great.*

"The bottom line is that once you get past the initial build out and marketing of your website, you should evaluate each acquisition channel against all of the others to see where budget should be allocated to grow the business."

I looked up at Dave. "You're right. We are going to be in trouble with Steve, and Raj."

Dave laughed out loud. "Don't think about how much trouble you'll be in. Think about how happy Joe will be that you've given him one metric that defines the performance of his business. Sometimes people don't like to face the truth, and our job as marketers is to look beyond basic marketing and analyze how the business as a whole is performing. If the answer is 'not well,' then we won't have our marketing jobs for very long."

I offered a weak smile. *Who knew how ruthless this whole marketing business could be? And here I thought it was all about writing catchy slogans and putting together beautiful websites.*

Turns out it's about all that—and a whole lot more.

✓ Always review and confirm your organization's business objectives before setting out to design a website or mobile app

✓ Key questions to ask when determining a website's objectives: Should it create awareness, generate leads or sales, highlight events and/or supply information?

✓ Determining the cost to generate each lead helps organizations set an appropriate budget for their marketing efforts, while also estimating potential profitability

✓ There are three categories of visitor that will come to a website — paid, owned, and earned

✓ An example of an owned property is your company's website

✓ Earned visitors tend to migrate to websites from social media or other channels in the form of likes, fans, followers, or referral traffic

✓ Paid traffic tends to derive mostly from Google Ad Words, Facebook ads, Twitter Cards, or other paid means of driving traffic to a website.

✓ The key to any successful search-focused content strategy is to make sure you're getting links from authoritative sites

✓ Google sees your website as a collection of pages, not a book that reads from start to finish

✓ Be prepared to track where leads are coming from, and to shift budget depending on what channel is the most successful

✓ There are six ways to acquire traffic: organically, directly, through referral, via social media, by email and through paid advertising

✓ Determining your customer Cost-per-Acquisition (CPA) on each channel will help determine return on advertising spend (ROAS)

✓ Once you build and market your website, you should evaluate each acquisition channel to determine where budget should be allocated to grow the business

Chapter 9

"The other thing we need to do well, of course, is build a great website," Dave pointed out.

Um, isn't that what we'd been discussing since I started?

"You might think that's what we've been discussing since day one," Dave interjected, "and we have." There he goes, reading my thoughts again.

"But now I want to get down to the basics, review some elements that every website must have. Would it surprise you to know that only a few are currently featured on DesignSpace's website?"

I shook my head. *We'd spent plenty of time discussing the cons of this company's current website.*

"The first is a homepage indicator," Dave said, circling back to something we'd discussed on my first day. "In order to have good, user-friendly navigation around your website, you need to give visitors an easy path back to your homepage. All too often, visitors click on a page only to find they can't navigate backwards. This forces them to start a new search, which leaves them with a really poor user experience, and can sometimes either push them back to a search engine or even to a competitor's website. Either way, traffic is being directed away from your site, and nobody wants that. To solve the problem, we'll need to include a homepage link or a hyperlinked logo that points back to the homepage."

"Got it," I said as I typed. "Any other must-haves?"

"Lots," replied Dave. "Google is a big fan of breadcrumbs, which are the lists across the top of the page that show you where you are in the navigation tree. From a machine perspective, this is an orderly hierarchy on the website, and you can go back to any particular level by clicking on the breadcrumb. From a user perspective, these simple little hyperlinks allow you to navigate much more easily."

"The third must-have for any website is an indication of its author. In a B2B situation, the author would most often be the company, foundation, or organization that's responsible for design and maintenance. This information is usually marked in the footer on each web page and often includes an About Us explanation of who the author is and what they do."

It's important to tell your website visitors who you are. Got it.

"But that's not all," Dave continued. "You should ideally have an indicator explaining the authorship of the particular page that the visitor is viewing. If it's an About Us or Contact Us page that's part of the main content, the author would most often be someone from the organization's marketing department. However, if you have a blog, news page, or newsletter page, the author of that particular section should be clearly indicated as well.

"And that brings us to our next must-have: a blog. While most websites have Contact Us or About Us pages that provide information about who owns the site and its purpose, as well as what the organization does, good websites also have entire blogs devoted to who they are and what they do. This provides much-needed credibility, as well as information. Blogs are another platform for posting thought leadership relevant to the company—for example, if one of this company's designers wanted to write about new trends in office furniture. Joe's current website doesn't really have enough of these important elements, and they're just some of the factors hurting DesignSpace's search engine rankings."

That and the fact that the current design is pretty much a disaster, I thought.

"When it comes to the Contact Us page, you not only need to have one, of course, but it also needs to contain the right information. It's really important to make it as simple as possible for customers to reach your organization if they want to make service or new sales inquiries. The types and amount of contact information needed depend on the type of website you're building. Customer service information is extremely important for websites that handle money, such as stores, banks, or credit card companies. That's because users need a fast and reliable way to ask questions or get help when a problem occurs." Dave took off his glasses, rubbing his eyes, then slipped them back on.

"Certain sites that are designed to separate you from your money in exchange for products or services need to have additional information to convey an adequate sense of trust and resources to assist their customers. Clearly stated policies on payment exchanges and returns are also important in helping to achieve better search engine rankings. Sometimes this information is listed on a specific Customer Service page; that's fine, as long as it's easily accessible."

"That all makes sense," I said. "I'm assuming that once this basic content is posted you don't have to worry about it again, right?"

"Quite the opposite, actually," Dave corrected. "One of our last website must-haves is regular maintenance. Not all pages have to be updated all the time, because some information, like you address and contact details, won't change on a regular basis. But other parts of the site should be updated regularly, especially because people often switch or jump between web browsers, while search engines are constantly scouring websites for new information to update their rankings."

"So does that mean updating the website daily, weekly, or maybe monthly?"

Dave paused and considered his answer. "That really depends on the organization in question. I would say that companies should update their content on an almost-daily basis, particularly B2C organizations. B2B-focused businesses could get away with updating every few days, but I wouldn't push it much further. The online marketplace moves quickly, so it's imperative to keep pace. As I mentioned, a blog is a great way to keep your website fresh, while your existing pages should change on a regular basis to update your product and service offerings, and, ideally, stay a step ahead of the competition."

"What's the final must-have?" I wondered out loud.

"That would be a responsive design," Dave answered. "As I mentioned before, that term simply means a website design that can be viewed well on any relevant device—mobile, tablet, or desktop. The amount of mobile traffic is growing every day, and companies that are serious about getting found online must have a strong mobile presence. A responsive website not only delivers a better user experience, but it takes into account the specifics of any and all relevant browsers. Probably more important, Google will penalize you for maintaining a mobile page that has limited functionality, or for having a non-mobile-friendly page that actually has more functionality. You have to be careful when upgrading to a mobile-friendly platform that the process is executed properly and the new website is optimized for the right browsers."

This made perfect sense to me. "You know, more than once I've sat on my couch with my phone in my hand, my iPad in my lap, and my laptop open on the coffee table in front of me, and I've searched for different information on each device."

"Then you're a pretty typical millennial." Dave smiled. "Unfortunately, I'm not in your generation, yet I do that, too. So do my wife and a lot of our friends. Viewing and web-surfing habits have changed dramatically over the years. People want information when they want it, and if that means using multiple devices at once, they'll do exactly that. Now, how obvious do you think the DesignSpace website's call to action needs to be to cut through all of that noise?"

"Um, I'd say pretty loud and clear."

"To say the least." Dave leaned back in his chair with his hands behind his head, then spoke in a tone that suggested he was thinking out loud.

"Since Joe wants us to optimize his website for monetary conversions, we need to discuss exactly what that means for potential customers who will visit this site."

"Okay," I said, willing to take the bait. "What exactly does that mean?"

Dave leaned forward and put his elbows on the table. "As I explained earlier, Google takes pages that can impact the future happiness, health, or wealth of its users very seriously. They closely inspect all of the elements of the main and supplementary content to make sure that the website is offering legitimate—and not potentially fraudulent—information to ensure the best possible end-user experience. In English, that means that if a website can separate you from your money, it has to live up to higher standards."

"I'd hate to see the standards that an online gambling site needs to live up to," I joked. Dave ignored my lame attempt at humor and kept talking.

"This is where third-party reviews are very important," he continued. "When products or services are expensive or represent a major investment, Google tries to highlight other websites that can validate the claims, and sales proposition, or the information being provided. You can see why it's important for websites to have a good reputation, an extensive customer service report, and a healthy collection of positive online reviews. Almost every website boasts about how good it is, but third-party reviews are what Google really cares about when trying to determine real customer experiences before assigning an appropriate search engine ranking."

"So," I said, keying notes as I talked, "you really have to care about what's being said about you online. Would that be fair to say?"

"Very fair," Dave answered.

"Okay, but what happens if you get a negative review online?"

"Good question. No business is perfect, and even the best customer service rep may have a bad day or provide a less-than-stellar customer experience. There are also people who are very, very picky, and would never rank somebody five out of five on customer service rating scale. They feel there is always some way that the customer experience could improve."

Dave smiled to himself. "I had a teacher like that back in the day and it drove me a little nuts," he recalled. "But Google realizes that the definition of what it means to have a great user experience will vary depending on the reviewer, so it tends to take an aggregate impression of indicators when assigning trust values to a website."

I thought back to my near-daily experiences at the Bean serving Tim, an egomaniac stock trader who insisted that his mocha chai soy latte be prepared in *EXACTLY THE RIGHT WAY*, all the way down to the drink's temperature. I could swear he carried a thermometer to the café each day to make sure his coffee was prepared to his exacting specifications. *He did always leave a nice tip, though, and that made his demands a little easier to stomach.*

"But let's get back to talking about user intent and what that means," Dave continued. "For Joe, there are three different types of intent to consider: *action intent, navigation intent, and information intent.*"

I sighed as I struggled to keep up with the flow of information. Dave and I had been working together long enough for him to pick up on my cue, and he took a few minutes to expand on his thoughts.

"A customer may be looking to buy a particular product that Joe carries," he explained. "That would be the *action intent*. Or they may be poking around the DesignSpace website to see if it offers a particular good or service; that would be a *navigation intent*. Or, they might be searching specifically for information about DesignSpace—which is, no surprise, *information intent*. When rebuilding a site, you have to take these three potential search intents into account and design pages to address each one."

Okay. Got it. Things were making sense.

"Let's take the navigation intent, or people searching for DesignSpace." Dave continued, "There are a number of different things you should do to make sure you're found first in the search results for your company. First and foremost is signing up for Google Webmaster Tools. This is a free service provided by Google that allows you to verify that you are the owner of a particular website. Ideally, you'd also want to verify this with an email address that's associated with your site—susan@designspace.com, for example—but that isn't necessarily required. A secondary consideration is setting up a Google My Business profile. This is Google's Yellow Pages–like directory. You can use it to provide information about store hours, photos of the business, a list of the products and services you offers, your geographic location, comments and reviews, and other important information. Having a verified listing with Google My Business will immediately provide relevancy and help establish a reputation online."

"Is that a free service as well?" I asked.

"Yep. All you need is a Google account and the time to set up the profile. It's really very simple. The third thing you should do is claim your listings on all of the major social networks. Facebook, Twitter, Instagram, and LinkedIn are all important trust indicators today, and more platforms will be just as important tomorrow. Sign up for each one of these social networks and set up a company page. Now, a lot of business owners will argue that they simply don't have the time to maintain a presence on each social media platform. I could debate the importance of doing exactly that, but for now it's important to remember that you don't have to be the most social butterfly in the world. At the very least, you should have a basic profile on each of the networks to make it easy for people to learn more about your business. You really need to think about your customers and their online or social media habits. You may not like Facebook, for example, but if all of your customers are there, then you have to have a presence there too."

I smiled. *I spend half of my waking hours on Facebook and Snapchat,* so I totally understood Dave's point. *My bigger challenge is getting off of Facebook, Twitter, Snapchat, Instagram, and YouTube. Tuning into these channels is definitely not a problem.*

"What about directory listings?" I asked.

"Absolutely, you want your information to be made widely available wherever people may be looking for you, but the information has to be consistent across all of the directories and you have to be prepared to customize the results," Dave stressed.

I nodded, but maybe not enthusiastically enough. It was so much to take in, and it had been a long day.

"I think it might be best if we called it a day," Dave said, staring down at his laptop before darting his eyes back in my direction.

"I'm okay to keep going," I said, doing some quick neck stretches and shoulder rolls. "We're in a bit of a rhythm, so we should probably just keep the momentum going, if you're happy to do that."

"I like your work ethic." Dave smiled. "Let's discuss a few more concepts and then finish up for today. That will also give me an extra day to sort out other business before I leave."

"Leave?"

"Did you not receive Joe's email? This part of my engagement with DesignSpace is about to end. I'm off to another couple of projects, but I'll be back in a month or so to check on your progress, do some website testing, and help tie up any loose ends."

"Wait a minute . . . you're saying that I'm about to be flying solo?" I said with a bit of panic creeping into my voice.

"That's right. Joe asked me if I thought you were ready, and I told him that I definitely felt you were up to the task. So, yes, you are going to be flying solo."

Well, this job was great while it lasted. My heart sank as I thought about trying to rebuild a website basically on my own, with Dave off doing other projects with other clients. *How in the world was I going to pull this off?*

"You might be wondering how you're going to pull this off," Dave started.

No, really—I think this guy's telepathic.

"You have all the tools you need. You're ready to do the job. If you get stuck, you just need to review your notes and use your best judgment. You'll do fine. As it is, you already have a pretty solid knowledge of website design requirements. You have a good background in search and user intent, and knowing about that puts you well ahead of a lot of the marketers that I've worked with over the years. And I'm not exaggerating to boost your confidence."

"Well, you've definitely given me a lot to think about," I said, still slightly dejected.

"I definitely have. There are just a few more things to cover before we wrap up. The first is that you should really learn more about DesignSpace's customers by looking at how well the site performs for each user query, then come up with some ideas on how it can be improved. I have to head out for a few hours, but when I get back, I'm good to work late and review this with you before I give you some pointers on designing a website brief. Sound good?"

As good as it's going to get, I thought.

Dave packed up his laptop and headed out. Intrigued by what I was learning—but more than a little weary—I spent the next few hours back at my desk entering search queries and trying to learn as much as I could about our clients, just as Dave had recommended. It wasn't long before I started seeing patterns and highlighting much-needed areas of improvement.

I finally took a break and headed down to one of the six Starbucks within a block's radius for a caffeine pick-me-up. When I got back to my desk, there was a note from Dave, letting me know he was back. I gathered my things and made my way, once again, to the boardroom.

"How did it go?" Dave asked.

"Good," I said, without much conviction. "But I think I've got my work cut out for me."

Dave raised an eyebrow. "Oh?"

I looked across the table at him, nodded, then glanced back down at my laptop screen. "I took a look at the data for the DesignSpace website, and even though I'm not overly familiar with Google Analytics, I can see that the site is posting some pretty terrible performance metrics."

"I see," Dave said, leaning in. "What metrics led you to that conclusion?"

"The first graphic that you see in the dashboard shows website traffic.

At the moment, the site only gets a few dozen hits per day. I know that we're a B2B-focused company and that our traffic will be lower because of our business model, but I'm guessing that our competitors get hundreds of hits every day, if not more."

"So the phone is ringing off the hook and orders are flowing in to those websites with all the traffic, right?" Dave asked.

I shook my head. "I can't comment on what our competitors are doing, but in our case, even though we're getting some calls based on that weak website traffic, our conversion rate from visitors to leads is pretty dismal. It's really frustrating to see that happen. Ideally, we should be converting a lot more of our website visitors into customers."

Dave smiled. "It looks like you have two problems—traffic, or the lack thereof, and poor conversions. Does that sound fair?"

"I think that's pretty fair to say."

"Then it looks like you do have your work cut out for you. Did you get the email I sent with contact details for Alicia Suarez, the web designer?"

"I saw that one. I haven't had a chance to reach out to her yet. I know Joe wants to use her services, but I wasn't quite sure yet where to start or what information to give her so she could get to work."

"Not a problem," Dave remarked as he stood up and began his usual think-pace routine. "Before you begin any website redesign initiative, it's crucial to put together a website brief for your designer. Consider it a roadmap for them to follow that sets your expectations and outlines your requirements as a business. It's one of the most important parts of this whole process."

"Tell me more, I'm all ears," I said, fingers poised above my keyboard.

"Even better, I'll show you." My email chimed and, sure enough, there was another document from Dave, this one labeled "Website Brief Tips."

A website brief is an important document that explains your website requirements to a designer/developer in significant detail. It should contain two main sections:

Company Information

In this section, make sure to answer the following questions:

- What does your company do?
- Who does it serve?
- What products/services does it make?
- What are its value propositions?
- What is its competitive advantage?
- Who are the main competitors in the marketplace?

The Challenge and the Opportunity

This section outlines your current website's shortcomings—that could be a lack of sales or traffic, for example—and what needs to change. Are any components of the website salvageable, or does it need to be rebuilt from scratch? Do you need to develop an entirely new brand identity as part of the project (for example, logo, web copy, etc.)? This section should answer several other important questions:

What is the website's purpose (e.g., inform, sell, etc.)? Who will it target (outline demographic information if possible)?

What are your short- and long-term goals for the website?

What content will need to be developed for the website and who will be responsible for producing it?

Approximately how many pages and other elements will you require as part of this project (e.g., e-commerce, social media, blogging, client login, etc.)

What kind of content-management system will you require? Would you prefer to use an open-source platform such as Drupal or WordPress? Something else? (If your team doesn't include someone with HTML experience, we recommend including an open-source content-management system.)

What is the timeline for completion?

"This is just a quick summary assumes that you've already chosen your designer or design firm," Dave continued as I scanned the new cheat sheet. "It's not about how to write a request for proposals or assess submissions. It also assumes you've discussed pricing with your supplier, which is a major consideration since web development fees can really vary. Anyway, I thought I'd spare you the boredom of having to review all of those other considerations right now. I think you have enough on your plate at the moment, so we'll save that discussion for another time."

"That's a really helpful summary, thanks," I said. "I'll think about these points and prepare something to send to Alicia. Have you worked with her many times in the past?"

"We've worked together mainly on a freelance basis, but for about five years. She's very talented, extremely creative, and her fees are reasonable. Those are important characteristics in a good web designer. Oh, and she delivers her work on time and on budget. A lot of her competitors miss the mark on at least a few of those points."

I glanced at my screen; it was getting close to eight o'clock. Dave closed the lid on his laptop and stood up.

"So, this is the end of the road for a little while, I guess. Even though I'm going to be working with other clients, I'll still be accessible by phone or email if you have any questions."

"I was pretty worried before," I replied, "but I have your outline on writing a website brief, and all of the other information you've given me over the last few days. I think I'll be okay. I might even enjoy myself!"

"I *know* you'll enjoy it," he said. "In fact, I know you're going to do an incredible job. Don't worry if you make a mistake along the way; that's part of the learning curve. And don't forget to start working on website content while Alicia starts building out the site. A lot of website launches get delayed due to a lack of content."

"I will."

And with that, Dave walked over and shook my hand. He wished me luck and then he left. I was on my own, but I finally felt confident that I could get the job done.

Now, I had to build a website.

✓ Website pages should include hyperlinked logos or Back buttons to allow for easier navigation

✓ Google likes to see breadcrumbs at the top of web pages. These are lists across the top of a page that show users where they are in the navigation tree

✓ Always be sure to include author information on web pages, typically in a page footer

✓ Include contact information on a Customer Service or Contact Us page. This helps users acquire information with ease

✓ Website content should be updated regularly because people often switch or jump between web browsers, while search engines are constantly scouring websites for new information to update their rankings

✓ Websites must be responsive, meaning they are viewable on any digital device—mobile, tablet, or desktop

✓ To ensure peak search performance for your company, Use Google Webmaster, set up a Google My Business profile and include listings on all major search engines

Chapter 10

The next six weeks saw a hectic flurry of emails between me and Alicia. Almost immediately after receiving my brief, Alicia asked for additional information on the DesignSpace brand. I had included as much information as possible, but she asked me to delve deeper, thinking about design concepts and how we wanted the company to be positioned not just now but a few years into the future. I quickly learned just how important that is to the success of a project like a website rebuild.

The technical side was another major concern given the fact that we wanted to add everything from an office design engine—that would allow clients to virtually insert our office furniture into their workspaces—to a really user-friendly content-management system. For the latter, we narrowed the field down to two website platforms, Drupal and WordPress. In the end, we went with WordPress due to its frequent updates and minimal learning curve.

Alicia sent over several website design mood boards that I presented to Joe. Together we decided on a brand direction and feel that was clean, contemporary, and, in my opinion, pretty sophisticated. We even worked together to select the right images. Going in, I had no idea it would be such an involved process. At the same time, though, I convinced Joe that we should take the opportunity to do a brand refresh. Alicia had a ton of experience developing brand identities, and it made sense to tap into her expertise.

He agreed, but asked me to oversee the process while he was away at a trade show, then off for a two-week vacation.

"I trust you," he reassured me. "Have a pleasant surprise ready when I get back in three weeks."

"Are you *sure*? Remember, this is my first time handling this sort of thing . . . "

"That's why I hired you. You have my full confidence."

Good thing I was feeling more confident myself, otherwise there's no way I could have pulled this off. And thank goodness for Alicia! It helped being able to work with someone as experienced and competent as she is.

Within a week, she produced a new logo and brand guidelines, and I worked on the website copy with a writer she recommended. I asked the writer to keep the tone of the copy in line with the style direction for the website itself—friendly, yet professional; sophisticated yet accessible. I thought he did a great job. Or at least I hoped he did. I still had to present the final product to Joe for approval.

Finally, after seemingly endless back-and-forths with both Alicia and the writer, I had something to show Joe. Now all I had to do was get him to give the thumbs-up so we could set a date to launch the new website. Soon enough, Joe was back from vacation and wandering the office, greeting everyone before slipping into the boardroom to start a series of meetings. I was up first; it was time to show off my digital handiwork.

"How was your vacation?" I asked as I entered the room and set my laptop down on the table.

"Amazing," he said. "There's nothing better than relaxing in the south of France. The family had a great time and I'm rested and ready to get back to work."

I really need to start my own company, I thought. *I, too, could use some time in the south of France—like maybe wandering the coastline in Nice or Cannes for a week. A girl can dream, can't she?*

"Glad you had a good time," I said. "I have a website and new branding to show you."

I connected my laptop to the overhead projector and dimmed the lights in the room. I filled Joe in on how I'd approached the design aspect of the project with Alicia, helping her to better understand the Design-Space brand, his business objectives, and how we should be positioned in the industry.

I toggled through each page of the new site explaining various decisions, showing off the cool features, and breaking down each design element with care. Joe sat silently, watching with a poker face. I could feel myself breaking out in a nervous sweat.

He hates it. I've wasted all this time and money. I'm going to get fired. No question.

"I have only one question," he stated sternly. "Why didn't you send me this while I was on vacation?"

"Um, I guess because you were away and I figured you wanted to relax."

"Well, I would have liked to have seen it sooner." Joe's expression was the picture of disappointment . . . before a sly smile crept across it. "It's absolutely perfect! You hit a total homerun. Congratulations, Susan! I'll give the copy a closer proofread to make sure there aren't any typos or minor edits I'd like to make, but I think we have a winner. Today's Monday, so let's try to launch by Thursday and take a few days to look for any bugs before we send an email to our clients letting them know about the rebrand and relaunch. Sound good?"

I was stunned, speechless, silent. "Sh-sure," I said. The word could barely pry its way out of my mouth. Suddenly, a wave of pride swept over me. *I did it! I managed to produce gorgeous new branding and a website that should help our company sell more—and help people know, go, or buy, as Dave would put it.*

"I'll get right on it."

I stood up and walked out of the boardroom, completely dumbstruck. Making my way back to my desk, I passed Jim, our chief designer, who asked if I was okay. I suppose the stunned expression of my face made it seem as if I'd just been fired, or told that I had a week to live. In fact, I was happy—really, really happy.

"I'm good," I answered Jim. "In fact, I'm great."

I pulled out my phone and sent a text to Helen.

We're going out tonight. Saying NO is not an option.

She must have been bored at work because her reply came back in about ten seconds.

What happened this time?

My boss loved the website! I did it!

Wasn't that what you were hired to do in the first place?

Don't be such a buzz-kill!! Meet me at Fluid at 8.

Done.

The next morning I hauled myself into the office. The previous night's festivities had left my head feeling as if it was full of rocks. I would have snuck under my desk and hidden for the day, had that been an option. I'd proved once and for all that too much of a good thing can be really bad—in this case, too many glasses of a very nice Australian shiraz.

I opened my laptop and checked my email, praying that I could float through the day doing little or no work.

That's when I noticed the email from Dave:

I hear you did an incredible job on the website! Great work. I'm really happy for you. Knew you could do it. Are you free on December 6th at around 11 a.m.? I know I'm asking way in advance, but I know you're busy and I wanted to book your time while I could. By then I'll have finished the current project I'm working on. I want to review a few other concepts with you before I start working with another client. Let me know.

I responded right away, saying that I was free, then set out to learn more about website testing before idling over to the coffee machine and jacking myself up on caffeine. This was going to be a very long day.

A few months passed and all was going well with the website. Our traffic had grown dramatically and sales had increased by 15 percent—about halfway to our goal. I was at my desk researching some of our competitors' recent marketing initiatives when I looked up from my laptop and saw Dave.

"Hey, website expert. How's it going?"

"Really good. You?" I said smiling up at him.

"I'm good, as well. Are you ready for our meeting?"

"Sure. You head down and I'll meet you there."

I made my way to the boardroom and walked in as Dave was wiping his glasses. I took my usual seat and waited anxiously to start.

"I don't think I mentioned in my last email, but I want to talk about testing."

"I thought I was done with testing when I got out of university." I cracked.

"You're never done learning about how to improve your company's online activities." Dave smiled, acknowledging my joke. "To manage DesignSpace's online presence properly, you'll need to set up methods and processes to test everything. Now, you're probably wondering why I stayed away for longer than I'd originally planned. The first reason is that Joe told me you were doing a great job and didn't need any handholding. Knowing that, I wanted to give the new website a few months to start compiling analytics data for us to review together. Does that make sense?"

"It does."

"Good. I suppose the first thing to point out before we get moving is that your marketing efforts will—and should— change continuously in response to competitive pressures, shifting market conditions, and even client fatigue. Even B2B customers will get tired of seeing the same things on your website. What works for you today probably won't work tomorrow."

"That makes sense," I said. "But where do we begin?"

Dave pointed to my laptop. "You start with all that great data and tracking information you've collected by adding Google Analytics to the website. The objective is to identify the low-hanging fruit—the easiest opportunities with the largest potential gain. You're in a good position because Joe has given you free rein, and you can make all the changes you want within the budget he's given you. Not everyone is in that same boat. Often there are layers of management approval to go through—but I should slow down. I'm getting ahead of myself."

He paused for a moment to collect his thoughts. "Let's go back to the beginning. How you evaluate opportunities to improve all aspects of a website's performance depends on what success looks like to you. In this case, that means determining the specific action we're trying to get users to take on the site."

"I think it's fair to say this site is trying to accomplish a few different things," I responded. "There's an e-commerce component, but the site is also meant to generate leads and serve a brochure function for our office furniture and design services."

"Let's take a look at the e-commerce aspect first," Dave said. "It's easier to measure success there, since the only metric we're tracking in this case is purchases. We'll also take a look at our micro-conversions in a few minutes."

"Micro-conversions?" I asked.

"Yes. Those are the little actions that a website visitor takes that indicate interest but don't necessarily indicate an intention to make a purchase today. They just tell us these customers are on the e-commerce journey. They're moving down the funnel toward a purchase. An example would be signing up for a mailing list or asking to be sent a catalog. A form fill would also qualify, but that might be better categorized as a lead, depending on your goal."

"Okay," I said, somewhat confused. "I hate to ask again, but where do we start?"

Dave chuckled and acknowledged the challenge at hand. "We start by testing opportunities," he began. "We use DesignSpace's goals as our constant benchmark to evaluate success. Since Joe wants more revenue, that's where we'll start. We have to determine which pages have the highest potential to impact the organization's bottom-line performance. This is usually based on the pages' importance, and the ease with which we can change them. "For example, in Google Analytics, you can look at how many people added products to your cart, then abandoned the cart before completing the sale."

I looked up from my laptop. "But if there are a lot of abandoned carts, you should just fix the transaction process, right?"

Dave smiled at me again. "Yes, but that's why user experience and user friendliness are important factors when determining what to change. It may not be easy to change the cart; you might be using third-party software, or you could have integrated some back-end payment gateway that's expensive and a nightmare to change. I believe you've done the former, right?"

I nodded. "So I'm assuming you've got a plan?"

Who was I kidding? Dave always had a plan.

He laughed out loud this time. "Yes. We start with a cycle approach. But first, you have to understand that a website isn't a brochure that you print once and then leave sitting static for the rest of the year. It should be a living, breathing, adjusting sales tool that drives you toward your goal. The only way to ensure this is by having a plan in place to continuously improve your marketing and website performance. Here are the basic steps." He leaned back in his chair and counted off items on his fingers while I typed:

1. Analysis

2. Hypothesis

3. Plan test

4. Design and copywriting

5. A/B/N testing with tools

6. Monitor

7. Complete and summarize

8. Go back to Step 1

I ignored the fact that I didn't know what some of this stuff meant yet.

w Dave, and trusted he'd explain it all in good time. "I think I'm get-
g most of this now," I said. "But how do analytics fit into the picture?"

"Well, analytics software like Google's look at the number of visitors
and pages, then analyze the relationship between actions on that page.
They place a little tracking cookie on a visitor's computer to know whether or not they've been to that site before, and that analyzes where they've
gone on the site once they arrive. Remember, everything starts with the
page. A website is simply a collection of pages. Analytics tell you how a
particular page performs." On his own laptop, Dave had opened Google
Analytics and was looking at DesignSpace's dashboard. He turned the
screen to face me, and moved his chair around.

"The easiest thing is to determine which of your pages are landing or
exit pages."

"But I thought landing pages are mainly used in pay-per-click campaigns," I interjected.

Dave nodded. "They are. But from an analytics point of view, a landing page is simply the first page that a visitor sees when they arrive to
your site. Depending on how your site is designed, you may have similar
layouts, such as product category pages, or individual product pages. The
key thing to take into account is the behavior of visitors on similar pages
across the website. Your homepage may get the most overall visits and be
the top landing page, but if you have a template on your site for all your
category pages or all your product pages, when you combine them together
that style of page may actually be a more popular landing page than your
homepage. You can look for indicators like a high bounce rate—meaning
they bounced back off the site, or hit the Back button—or low conversion
rates to try to identify problem areas and poorly performing pages."

He pointed at another section in analytics, labeled "Exit Pages."

"An exit page is simply the last page on your site that a person views

prior to leaving the site," he explained. "Pages with a high exit rate in
that people either found what they were looking for, or were prevented
from finding what they were looking for in the first place and bounced o₁
These high landing and high exit pages can be a good place to start testing
changes to the site, but you have to be careful. Some pages are good exits,
such as after someone completes a form, but some are bad. Like halfway
through your checkout process. But first we need to create a hypothesis."

Aw crap. I thought I was done with chemistry when I left high
school.

"What do you mean?" I asked, dreading the answer.

"Now that you think you may have some pages to test based on
high bounce rate or high exit rate metrics—which are relatively easy to
change—let's go back to how the target pages relate to user intent. If the
target page happens to be a page on the path to making a purchase, does
it help or hinder the transaction? If the page is information based, does it
help or distract from the user intent?

"Next, we need to analyze the value proposition on each particular
page. What value does this page add to the user? DesignSpace is a B2B
service that's trying to offer something that nobody else does, and that
gives them an unfair advantage over their competitors. That's the value
proposition. The big question: Does the page have a clear explanation that
makes people understand almost instantly what it's about and what DesignSpace is offering?"

"Okay, I get it."

"Next, we have to look at relevance. How relevant is the particular
page for DesignSpace's clients? Does the problem that the page is designed
to solve clearly resonate in the minds of end users? If the problem isn't
relevant, then it's not going to cause any change in the behavior of people
who are visiting the site.

"You also have to take into account clarity," he added. "The clarity with which the information on the page is presented is very important in helping visitors understand that this particular solution completely addresses and solves their problem. One way to think about it is does the page tell them the action they should perform? Does it state the next step with no doubt as to what they should do?"

"So you need to make that really obvious from the outset," I said.

"That's right. You have to get inside your end-user's brain a little bit. What is their anxiety level? The greater the anxiety, the more likely they are to act, react, and take DesignSpace up on the offer to solve their challenges. You also have to look at their distraction level. Are they completely focused on trying to solve the problem that DesignSpace can solve, or did they accidentally stumble across the site while sitting on their couch with their phone while their children play in the background and the TV blares? How can this company's message penetrate such a high level of distraction?"

Speaking of distraction, at that moment I was listening to Dave, but also skimming my email to check for new messages. We millennials are multitaskers, after all. "Finally, we need to look at urgency," Dave added. "How urgent is the problem? Is it something that needs to be solved today, or is it something that can be addressed next week, next month, or at some undetermined point in the future? The more urgency you can include in your call to action, and the more of a prospect's hot buttons you can push, the more likely it is that they'll react positively to your products or services. In DesignSpace's case, most visitors won't have an urgent need to buy new office furniture, unless they're experiencing some sort of rapid growth. But for other companies, urgency is a major consideration."

"Got it," I said. "Ideally, you want to have a good value proposition that's highly relevant to your target audience and that's been clearly presented to an end user who may have a high level of anxiety but who is probably distracted and may or may not have an urgent need for the solution. Did I get it all?"

Dave laughed. "Absolutely! That was a great summary. Now that you know what it is we're trying to accomplish, we have to take a look at any particular page and try to form an opinion about what may or may not be impacting its performance. This is where forming a hypothesis comes into play."

I groaned. *There was just something about that word.*

"There's a reason why we think of this as scientific advertising," Dave continued. "Forming hypotheses about the shortcomings of a particular page or offer is very important in ensuring long-term success. So, how do you form a hypothesis, and what, exactly, is it? For today, consider it an educated guess around behaviors that we'll likely want to change, ones that will impact results positively. Then we'll do some testing to make sure that it does."

"Okay, let's talk hypotheses," I said.

"Let's start with a simple hypothesis that we can either prove or disprove," Dave said. "Let's say, for example, that we're thinking that our Add to Cart button should be changed to a contrast color and made more prominent. Our hypothesis might be: *Changing the button to a brighter color will result in a 30 percent improvement in e-commerce conversion rates within three months.* Or, let's say we wanted to completely modify a page and remove advertising from it. In that case, our hypothesis would be something like: *By removing advertising and making the site cleaner, we will improve our time-on-site metrics by 20 percent.* So the hypothesis structure is simply: *Changing X (the thing we want to change) into Y (the thing you want to change it into) will improve our conversion rate by Z (our conversion goal).*"

I looked at Dave. "Don't you think that's a bit much?"

Dave cocked his head and looked back at me. "What do you mean?"

I skimmed my notes quickly. "Well, it seems a little bit crazy to develop a theory about what may or may not be working on a page after the fact, then try to disprove it. Wait a minute." I paused. "That's exactly why we're doing this exercise, isn't it?"

Dave smiled. "Yes, we need something to prove or disprove so that we're not just making guesses about what may or may not work. So let's shift topics for a minute. A key element that is often overlooked—in addition to the need for a good, defined hypothesis—is a good plan for testing."

Right, back to high school we go.

"A good test is designed with a particular goal in mind. It should reflect the hypothesis, but it also needs to be carried out in an effective manner so that it doesn't carry on forever. When planning your test with a goal in mind, you should set a specific start date, along with some metrics that will indicate whether or not you've been successful. You should agree on these metrics before starting the test so there's no confusion or challenges once you've completed it."

"That makes sense. What's next?" I asked.

"Now we need to move to design and copywriting. One of the biggest mistakes you can make when improving a website's design is making too small a change. What's a small change? Well, it could be changing a button color here or some copy layout there. Changes like these may not be significant enough to make any kind of appreciable difference in your website's performance. I'm a big fan of big changes for big results. Change an element from one side of the page to the other, add some additional text, remove a button or change a slider—all of these represent pretty massive structural changes to a page and can be tested to deliver results relatively quickly."

"When in doubt, blow up the page and start over. Gotcha," I joked.

Dave laughed. "I'm glad you're paying attention! Let's move on to A/B/n testing with tools."

I help up my hand, signaling Dave to wait before moving on. "I can see a problem emerging in my future if I'm testing ten different pages at once," I said. "How on earth am I going to keep track of all of that information? You might have a thousand visitors here, another thousand visitors there. What can I do to avoid spending my whole day in Excel working on different spreadsheets?"

"First," Dave replied, "there are a lot of good tools out there that save you the hassle of doing exactly what you just described—and you're lucky, because that's exactly what we used to have to do. It doesn't matter which A/B testing tool you've decided to use, the important thing is to use one. These tools will enable you to make good decisions by evaluating the estimated success rates associated with any particular change. They'll let you know whether your new design has made a significant enough difference to be statistically relevant. I won't get into all the boring facts, but basically you're aiming for a 95 percent or higher statistical rate that the change you made will positively impact your results. Any of these tools will tell you once you've reached that level, but one of my favorites is Optimizely."

I quickly made a note to check them out later.

"Now, despite the fact that you're going to be using different tools, you should certainly monitor your results as they come in. If, for example, your change is negatively impacting results in a significant way, you want to address that as soon as possible. On the flipside, as soon as you reach a statistical significance that enables you to make a positive change, you should implement it and then start with another hypothesis before planning another round of testing. Thus, the testing cycle continues. It starts off with a hypothesis, goes through testing that evaluation, and gets you to a place where you can eventually infer what changes have and haven't worked before moving on to the next test."

I leaned back in my chair and glanced at my phone to check the time. Outside of the boardroom, I could see a few people making their way out of the office. "It's after one o'clock. Can we break for lunch?"

Dave laughed. "I think I've given you enough to think about for a little while. And besides, Joe didn't hire you to listen to me talk all the time. I just wanted to give you a bit more information to solidify the foundation you've already built as you work to improve DesignSpace's online presence. Once you've had the site running even longer and collect even more data, I'll sit down with you again and give you some pointers on what you should and shouldn't be doing to help the business continue to grow."

"Sounds good." I smiled. "Let's order some takeout so we don't waste time going out to eat."

I began a search for local Thai places—all the while looking for some of the important search engine marketing and optimization elements that I'd been taught earlier. By the time I'd found a spot, Dave was busy checking his email.

"Let me ask you," I said, "what do you think the Google of the future will look like?"

He thought for a moment before answering. "I would say that, in general, technology is going to impact everything. All of the things that we're doing right now are very important, but like every industry, this tech industry will eventually change, as well. What I'm telling you to do today is definitely a best practice right now, but that advice will surely change in the future. Mobile is huge, it is the future, but screen sizes will always be a major factor. Just keep in mind you need to stay a step ahead of key trends to maintain your online reputation with customers, which is paramount to your success. That said, I see Google moving toward intuitive, semantic results that will enable their machine to know what you need before you even know you need it. Each individual device and each individual person's preferences will be so ingrained into the user experience that our standard search engine results page won't even be needed."

"Wow, that would be a game-changer," I said.

"It would completely transform the user experience as we understand it today. Your devices will know your preferences inside and out. They may not know exactly what you're looking to do when you say something like, 'I want to get my nails done next Tuesday when I'm in Boston for a business meeting,' but Google will automatically know your itinerary. It won't know where you're going to be at what times, but it will schedule a driver to come and pick you up from your hotel three hours prior to your flight's departure time, for example. Google will let you know that it's booked your next nail appointment and will even take care of all the billing so it shows up on a monthly statement. The search and the need and the result will happen automatically. Eventually, Google will know what you need even before you need it."

Dave finished his predictions, stood up, and announced that he needed food. "I'm starving," he said.

"What you're describing is all a little scary, don't you think?" I wasn't quite ready to leave the topic yet.

"It's not scary if you know where the technology is going and bear in mind that this is the future. If you can plan for it, you'll be ahead of 99 percent of the people out there, and that's a very good thing—especially when you're a marketer."

I ordered lunch online and it arrived within thirty minutes. Dave and I sat in the boardroom, munching away on pad Thai and spring rolls and chatting mainly about business. When we finished eating, Dave slid his laptop into that beat-up leather satchel of his.

"Well, I guess this is it again," he said.

"What do you mean?"

"I've shared all of my secrets for website planning, and now you're on your own. And quite honestly, you don't need me anymore to do this again. When you're ready to start generating traffic and converting those clicks to more customers, have Joe reach out to me. There's another whole world out there for you to explore."

"You really know how to make an exit," I teased.

"I try to maintain an air of mystery with my work." He smiled.

Dave shook my hand as he'd done months earlier, wished me luck, and disappeared down the corridor, stopping briefly to say good-bye to Joe before leaving.

The feelings of anxiety I experienced the last time we parted ways were gone. He knew I was ready and so did I. I was officially a marketer now, and I knew I could handle most of DesignSpace's needs. Any services beyond my expertise could be outsourced to the network of suppliers that I'd managed to build since starting at the company. After all of my hard work, I finally knew that my future in this business was bright. And to think, I'd once been worried about building a "simple" website . . .

✓ Set up comprehensive testing processes and methods to better manage your company's online presence

✓ How you evaluate opportunities to improve all aspects of a website's performance depends on what success looks like to your company

✓ Micro-conversions are the small actions that a website visitor takes indicating potential interest in your brand

✓ Presenting website information in a clear and coherent way is critical to helping visitors understand that your company's solution will address and solve their problem

✓ The more urgency you can include in your call to action, and the more of a prospect's hot buttons you can push, the more likely it is that they'll react positively to your products or services

✓ A/B testing tools will enable you to make smart decisions by evaluating the estimated success rates associated with any particular change, and whether your new design has made a significant enough difference to be statistically relevant

Acknowledgments

This book would not be possible without the help and inspiration of the following people.

To my mother Brenda, and my late father, Doug. Thank you for the values, the trust, the faith and the drive to be better every day. Your excellent example of what a family would, could, and should be has enabled me to live an amazing life. Thank you for being hard on me when I needed it, for being supportive when I really needed it, and for always being there no matter how tough the path I chose.

To Chris Atchinson, my companion on this journey. This book would not be here if not for your amazing talent and ability to interpret, refine, and help me down the path to becoming an author. Your ability to translate my gibberish into a cohesive story, and to challenge my thinking is amazing. I truly could not have done it without you.

To Lisa Charters, who's generous guidance is truly awe-inspiring. Your vast experience has proven priceless, and the amazing people you introduced to me is worth more than I can say. Hopefully one day I will be able to return the favor and prove to be even a fraction as generous and valuable to you as you have been to me.

To Linda Pruessen and Tanya Back. Your ability to take a rough carving, shine it polish it, and turn it into something that I can truly be proud of is awesome to behold. Thank you for your help in getting this book into the hands of the people who can most benefit from it.

To my EO forum members both past and present who have been a part of this journey and so generous with their time: Craig Smith, Mauro Lollo, Frank Pitsikalis, David Levy, Kevin Leflar, Chris Hughes, Karen Brookman, David Foster, Ron White, Desiree Mathias, Brent Gingrich, Greg Woo, Jay Bousada, Hyman Ngo, David Farnell, Shane Bennett, and Blake Jarrett. Your insights, support and contributions have been invaluable. Many of your contributions have found their way onto these pages and for that I am grateful.

To Khalid Essam, thank you for always having my back, for making my work life easier, and for helping me free up the time and space to write this book. You are truly a pleasure to work with.

To Warren Rustand, thank you for being such an inspiration and helping me develop the discipline to finish this project and many others. Thank you for teaching me the value of having a balanced life, with personal, family, business and community all being equal contributors to the person I want to become. You are an inspiration to me, and I am grateful for our time together.

To all the people who have been, or are a part of, the AOK Marketing team. These have been the best 17 years of my life, and I can hardly wait to see what the next 100 bring.

To my clients, thank you for the privilege of working with you and for allowing me to share some of my experience in this book. What I have learned from you over the years has been one of my greatest gifts.

To you, the reader of this book. If you can glean one, or even two small things from these pages that will enable you to sell more, be more, and get closer to living your dreams, then I will have accomplished my goal. Thank you for taking this journey with me.

Finally to my beautiful wife Mary, and our kids, Mark and Christina. Thank you for filling my life with purpose and joy. I love you always and forever.

www.ingramcontent.com/pod-product-compliance
Lightning Source LLC
Chambersburg PA
CBHW060611210326
41519CB00014B/3628